Reading *for a* Bright Future

Abhay Joshi

Photo: ©Tamotsu Fujii

NAN'UN-DO

This Book is devoted to my parents and to my absolute soul.

Introduction

"Reading for a Bright Future" is a textbook combining in-built critical thinking skills with language skills. This book contains 17 carefully selected topics we may need to deal with in or during our professional life cycle. Each unit starts with pre-reading questions, thoughts about the topics, and has related vocabulary, listening, and writing activities. For every alternate lesson, crosswords are added for fun. Audio is included so students can listen to each reading passage and listening exercise.

This book would never have been completed without the help of Meghana Shrotri. Her timely guidance and cooperation are invaluable, which helped me to achieve this book. In addition, the Author is very grateful to Prof. Dar Watson for building a unique questionnaire in the book. Special thankfs to Prof. Dr. M. Nishimura, who helped check the book's contents periodically to make it practical for new generations. Tamotsu Fuji who doesn't really need an introduction—The legend who has photographed almost all well known personas, generously gifted me his photographs! I am more than indebted to him for this gesture of his, which has taken my book to such a high scale.

The Author sincerely believes that if someone had shared wisdom with him in his early 20s, as are **the contents of this book**, he would have made his life decisions much more wisely, and his life would indeed have been much more prosperous, hence, the whole purpose of bringing forth this book for the future generations.

How to Use This Book

Each photograph has a deep meaning, which is an excellent opportunity for the reader to think.

This exercise has five carefully designed questions to introduce the topic and cover the matter entirely. The activity prompts the students to start thinking about the case, and they can do so in pairs, small groups, or as a class at large. These questions are framed to let students know "what they do not know." When one does not know anything about a given topic, raising appropriate questions to gain knowledge reflects one's intellect. Teaching them this technique of raising such questions is an additional motive here.

This exercise has three statements closely related to the topic, enabling the students to express their views. They are encouraged to take a definite stand here.

Above the article is a headphone logo. Next is a tracking number denoting the track on the audio where students can listen and practice the intonation, which is a feature of pronunciation and contentions.

Each unit begins with a Topic sentence. In addition, each paragraph begins with a topic sentence for an easy and quick grasp of the topic.

The heart of each unit is an article about a topic related to life lessons. These life lessons may be from lifestyle, education, career, business, or worldly awareness. One may not face these challenges now. However, one is likely to encounter them at the coming turn or the next. Similarly, one may not face them all but most of them. Hence, the learnings are to be gathered now.
Each article is about 500 words created from a theoretical point of view, abiding by norms like the use of simple, assertive sentences and exciting language. Easy flow is ensured throughout the article. The author tries to give a complete picture by providing the pros and cons of every topic, and a practical message at the end of the article enhances its richness.

Listening practice from pp 111 & onwards.

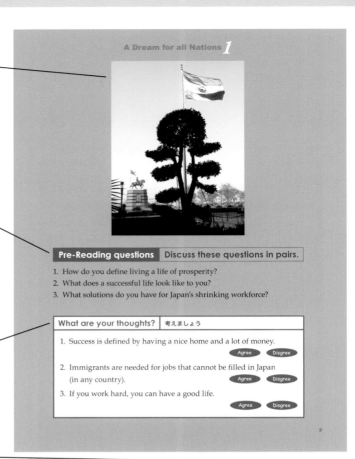

A Dream for all Nations *1*

Pre-Reading questions | **Discuss these questions in pairs.**

1. How do you define living a life of prosperity?
2. What does a successful life look like to you?
3. What solutions do you have for Japan's shrinking workforce?

What are your thoughts?	考えましょう

1. Success is defined by having a nice home and a lot of money.
   Agree   Disagree

2. Immigrants are needed for jobs that cannot be filled in Japan (in any country).
   Agree   Disagree

3. If you work hard, you can have a good life.
   Agree   Disagree

20 Y / M / D

A Dream for all Nations

The "American Dream" was, is and will continue to be the driving force of economic success in the United States. Arguably, this is the first nation founded on the monumental idea that "all men are created equal." In 1776, the Founding Fathers promised life, liberty, and the pursuit of happiness to many immigrants.

The meaning of the American Dream has changed over time. By the 1930s, it meant a successful career, home ownership, upward mobility, and wealth. Essentially, it represented equal opportunity regardless of family history or social status. For those willing to work hard, a good life was attainable.

The Lehman shock of 2008 impacted the meaning of the American Dream. It became less about accumulating wealth and more about living a meaningful life. Time spent with friends and family creating warm memories became the cornerstones of a fulfilling life.

In the 21st century, many believe prosperity and success are no longer easily achievable. Expensive housing and rising healthcare and higher education costs make upward mobility and wealth challenging to achieve. Others believe that the American Dream remains alive. Baby Boomers define this dream as having a large house and the financial means to raise a family. Generation X sees it as achieving professional success based on knowledge, wisdom and a well-paying job with benefits. Millennials view the American Dream as enjoying their lives by pursuing a passion and focusing less on consumerism.

Many countries, such as Japan, have the opportunity to create their own version of the American Dream by thinking outside the box. Indeed, the immigration of highly skilled labor is a promising solution to Japan's shrinking workforce due to the country's aging population. Japan's low crime rates, high quality of life, and rich culture make it an attractive place to live and raise a family. Therefore, the aspiration of living a happy life can be reproduced in any part of the world that welcomes immigrants searching for a better life.

Follow your bliss and the universe will open doors for you where there were only walls.

Joseph Campbell

A Dream for all Nations *1*

Vocabulary List. （辞書必要、必ず辞書を参照してください）

No.	Word	Definition	Definition in my language	Synonyms
1	monumental (adj.)			grand, great
2	mobility (n.)			movement
3	status (n.)			place, position
4	accumulate (v.)			gain, increase
5	cornerstone (n.)			essential
6	prosperity (n.)			wealth
7	benefit (n.)			aid, assistance
8	consumerism (n.)			consumption
9	reproduce (v.)			copy, recreate
10	immigrant (n.)			foreigner

Definition

a. an important foundation on which something is built
b. to increase over time
c. a position of someone when compared to other people in society
d. very great or important
e. successful; often by making a lot of money
f. money that is paid by a company when an employee needs medical care.
g. a person who comes to a country to live there
h. spending a lot of money on goods and services
i. to move from one position to another position
j. to make a copy of something

> After each article, a vocabulary list of 10-12 words from the unit is given, including their meanings and synonyms. It is shown in the tabular form, facilitating students to write the meanings in their mother tongue, ensuring a better understanding of English.

Vocabulary Review

Fill in the blanks with the words from the box below. Change the form of the words if necessary.

1. monumental	2. mobility	3. status	4. accumulate
5. cornerstone	6. prosperity	7. benefit	8. consumerism
9. reproduce	10. immigrant		

1. The scientist wants to _____ the results of the experiment.
2. The rich and famous live a life of _____.
3. Rice is the _____ of the Japanese diet.
4. The King and Queen of Britain are of high _____.
5. My father's _____ paid for my doctor's visit.
6. _____ is attainable to those that work hard.
7. Many _____ live in the United States and Germany.
8. The completion of the pyramids in Egypt was a _____ accomplishment.
9. My grandparents have _____ many things over the years.
10. Her _____ has decreased after breaking her leg playing soccer.

Idioms about *A Dream for all Nations*

Idioms	meaning
dream come true	something you really wanted has come true
a clean slate	to forget about past problems; to start from the beginning
to turn over a new leaf	to start behaving in a better way

Please choose the correct idioms from above

1. Making the Olympic team this year would be a _____.
2. Let's start on _____. It's all water under the bridge.
3. I promise I will _____ and will be more responsible.

Interesting facts (A Dream for all Nations)

1. A white picket fence is a well-known symbol of the American Dream.
2. The idea of the American Dream has motivated millions to immigrate to the US.
3. Austrian born Arnold Schwarzenegger immigrated to the United States hoping to become a celebrity and get rich. He did both.

> To master vocabulary, Fill in the blanks is included, in which the sentences are designed to be simple, short, and from everyday context. The words are laid out for easy selection/copying.

> Idioms form an integral part of American life/the English language. Volumes can be expressed in very few words using idioms/phrases. Hence, a few expressions are thoughtfully made a part of the article. Three essential idioms of these appear in the exercise section and their meanings in simple words. Fill in the blanks of three simple sentences. From day-to-day reference, are given, and appropriate idioms need to be chosen.

> Interesting facts about each article are stated to make learning and retention easy and exciting.

How to Use This Book

This exercise contains five multiple-choice questions to test comprehension of the article/ topic. All the five questions are why questions (e.g., what, where, which, how) covering the various aspects of the topic. They are aimed to develop an understanding of cause-effect relationships or reasoning skills. The first question in each set checks to understand the main idea.

Writing about the article is meant to develop expression in the English language; therefore, the answers are expected to be sentences long. For help, the beginning is done for the students. For better comprehension, repetition is avoided. All three questions use various 'wh' types, and the second question here is typical of the listing type for developing easy descriptive writing.

For every alternative lesson crosswords are added to give vocabulary practice.
By play way method

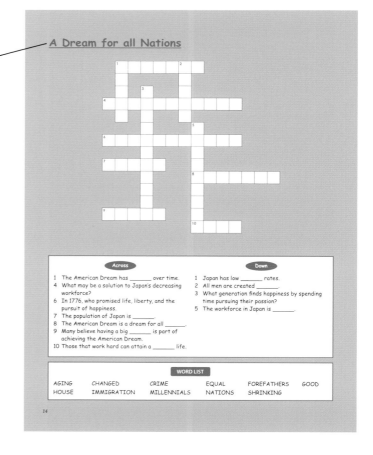

A Dream for all Nations *1*

Check your Understanding
Answer the following questions about the reading passage.

1. What is the main idea?
   (a) The American Dream is a cornerstone of US society even now
   (b) Immigration is the solution to Japan's shrinking workforce
   (c) Anyone that works hard can achieve the American Dream
2. When did the American Dream become less about consumerism?
   (a) During the Baby Boomer generation
   (b) In the 1930s
   (c) After the Lehman shock of 2008
3. Where can the American Dream be reproduced?
   (a) Anywhere in the world where people are living happily
   (b) Only in Washington D. C.
   (c) When visiting Disneyland
4. Why did the American Dream change over time?
   (a) The Civil War destroyed the American Dream
   (b) People began to view success and prosperity in different ways
   (c) Immigrants stopped coming to the United States
5. Who can achieve the American Dream?
   (a) Only immigrants living in the United States
   (b) Anyone working hard towards having a better life
   (c) Americans that are living in other countries

Writing about the Article
Answer each question based on the reading passage.

1. In this lesson, what is the meaning of prosperity?

2. How does each generation define the American Dream?
   Baby Boomers –

   Generation X –

   Millennials –

3. Why is Japan considered a nice place to live and raise a family?

13

A Dream for all Nations

Across
1 The American Dream has _____ over time.
4 What may be a solution to Japan's decreasing workforce?
6 In 1776, who promised life, liberty, and the pursuit of happiness.
7 The population of Japan is _____.
8 The American Dream is a dream for all _____.
9 Many believe having a big _____ is part of achieving the American Dream.
10 Those that work hard can attain a _____ life.

Down
1 Japan has low _____ rates.
2 All men are created _____.
3 What generation finds happiness by spending time pursuing their passion?
5 The workforce in Japan is _____.

WORD LIST

| AGING | CHANGED | CRIME | EQUAL | FOREFATHERS | GOOD |
| HOUSE | IMMIGRATION | MILLENNIALS | NATIONS | SHRINKING | |

14

CONTENTS

Japanese Translation
Yuta Tamaki &
Dr. Keisuke Kamimura

このテキストの音声を無料で視聴（ストリーミング）・ダウンロードできます。自習用音声としてご活用ください。
以下のサイトにアクセスしてテキスト番号で検索してください。

https://nanun-do.com　テキスト番号　［ **512158** ］

※ 無線 LAN（WiFi）に接続してのご利用を推奨いたします。

※ 音声ダウンロードは Zip ファイルでの提供になります。
　 お使いの機器によっては別途ソフトウェア（アプリケーション）
　 の導入が必要となります。

※ Reading for a Bright Future 音声ダウンロードページは以下の
　 QR コードからもご利用になれます。

Read by
Shizuka Anderson
Jack Merluzzi

Indian flag and Japanese Bonsai

Pre-Reading questions | Discuss these questions in pairs.

1. How do you define living a life of prosperity?
2. What does a successful life look like to you?
3. What solutions do you have for Japan's shrinking workforce?

What are your thoughts?	考えましょう

1. Success is defined by having a nice home and a lot of money.

    Agree   Disgree

2. Immigrants are needed for jobs that cannot be filled in Japan
    (in any country).

    Agree   Disgree

3. If you work hard, you can have a good life.

    Agree   Disgree

A Dream for all Nations

The "American Dream" was, is and will continue to be the driving force of economic success in the United States. Arguably, this is the first nation founded on the monumental idea that "all men are created equal." In 1776, the Founding Fathers promised life, liberty, and the pursuit of happiness to many immigrants.

5 The meaning of the American Dream has changed over time. By the 1930s, it meant a successful career, home ownership, upward mobility, and wealth. Essentially, it represented equal opportunity regardless of family history or social status. For those willing to work hard, a good life was attainable.

The Lehman shock of 2008 impacted the meaning of the American Dream. It became less about 10 accumulating wealth and more about living a meaningful life. Time spent with friends and family creating warm memories became the cornerstones of a fulfilling life.

In the 21st century, many believe prosperity and success are no longer easily achievable. Expensive housing and rising healthcare and higher education costs make upward mobility and wealth challenging to achieve. Others believe that the American Dream remains alive. 15 Baby Boomers define this dream as having a large house and the financial means to raise a family. Generation X sees it as achieving professional success based on knowledge, wisdom and a well-paying job with benefits. Millennials view the American Dream as enjoying their lives by pursuing a passion and focusing less on consumerism.

Many countries, such as Japan, have the opportunity to create their own version of the 20 American Dream by thinking outside the box. Indeed, the immigration of highly skilled labor is a promising solution to Japan's shrinking workforce due to the country's aging population. Japan's low crime rates, high quality of life, and rich culture make it an attractive place to live and raise a family. Therefore, the aspiration of living a happy life can be reproduced in any part of the world that welcomes immigrants searching for a better life.

Follow your bliss and the universe will open doors for you where there were only walls.

Joseph Campbell

Vocabulary List.　(辞書必要、必ず辞書を参照してください)

No.	Word	Definition	Definition in my language	Synonyms
1	monumental (adj.)		記念碑的な	grand, great
2	mobility (n.)			movement
3	status (n.)			place, position
4	accumulate (v.)			gain, increase
5	cornerstone (n.)			essential
6	prosperity (n.)			wealth
7	benefit (n.)			aid, assistance
8	consumerism (n.)			consumption
9	reproduce (v.)			copy, recreate
10	immigrant (n.)			foreigner

Definition

a. an important foundation on which something is built

b. to increase over time

c. a position of someone when compared to other people in society

d. very great or important

e. successful; often by making a lot of money

f. money that is paid by a company when an employee needs medical care

g. a person who comes to a country to live there

h. spending a lot of money on goods and services

i. to move from one position to another position

j. to make a copy of something

Vocabulary Review

Fill in the blanks with the words from the box below. Change the form of the words if necessary.

1. monumental	2. mobility	3. status	4. accumulate
5. cornerstone	6. prosperity	7. benefit	8. consumerism
9. reproduce	10. immigrant		

1. The scientist wants to _____ the results of the experiment.

2. The rich and famous live a life of _____.

3. Rice is the _____ of the Japanese diet.

4. The King and Queen of Britain are of high _____.

5. My father's _____ paid for my doctor's visit.

6. _____ is attainable to those that work hard.

7. Many _____ live in the United States and Germany.

8. The completion of the pyramids in Egypt was a _____ accomplishment.

9. My grandparents have _____ many things over the years.

10. Her _____ has decreased after she broke her leg playing soccer.

Idioms about *A Dream for all Nations*

Idioms	Meaning
dream come true	something you really wanted has come true
a clean slate	to forget about past problems; to start from the beginning
to turn over a new leaf	to start behaving in a better way

Please choose the correct idioms from above.

1. Making the Olympic team this year would be a _____.

2. Let's start on _____. It's all water under the bridge.

3. I promise I will _____ and will be more responsible.

Interesting facts (A Dream for all Nations)

1. A white picket fence is a well-known symbol of the American Dream.

2. The idea of the American Dream has motivated millions to immigrate to the US.

3. Austrian born Arnold Schwarzenegger immigrated to the United States hoping to become a celebrity and get rich. He did both.

Check your Understanding

Answer the following questions about the reading passage.

1. What is the main idea?
   (a) The American Dream is a cornerstone of US society even now
   (b) Immigration is the solution to Japan's shrinking workforce
   (c) Anyone that works hard can achieve the American Dream

2. When did the American Dream become less about consumerism?
   (a) During the Baby Boomer generation
   (b) In the 1930s
   (c) After the Lehman shock of 2008

3. Where can the American Dream be reproduced?
   (a) Anywhere in the world where people are living happily
   (b) Only in Washington D. C.
   (c) When visiting Disneyland

4. Why did the American Dream change over time?
   (a) The Civil War destroyed the American Dream
   (b) People began to view success and prosperity in different ways
   (c) Immigrants stopped coming to the United States

5. Who can achieve the American Dream?
   (a) Only immigrants living in the United States
   (b) Anyone working hard towards having a better life
   (c) Americans that are living in other countries

Writing about the Article

Answer each question based on the reading passage.

1. In this lesson, what is the meaning of prosperity?

2. How does each generation define the American Dream?
   Baby Boomers –

   Generation X –

   Millennials –

3. Why is Japan considered a nice place to live and raise a family?

A Dream for all Nations

Across

1 The American Dream has _____ over time.
4 What may be a solution to Japan's decreasing workforce?
6 In 1776, who promised life, liberty, and the pursuit of happiness.
7 The population of Japan is _____.
8 The American Dream is a dream for all _____.
9 Many believe having a big _____ is part of achieving the American Dream.
10 Those that work hard can attain a _____ life.

Down

1 Japan has low _____ rates.
2 All men are created _____.
3 What generation finds happiness by spending time pursuing their passion?
5 The workforce in Japan is _____.

WORD LIST

AGING   CHANGED   CRIME   EQUAL   FOREFATHERS   GOOD
HOUSE   IMMIGRATION   MILLENNIALS   NATIONS   SHRINKING

Pre-Reading questions | Discuss these questions in pairs.

1. Why do you think people choose to leave their countries to work?
2. What is brain circulation?
3. What sacrifices do people make that migrate to other countries?

What are your thoughts? | 考えましょう

1. Having a college education makes it easier to find work in another
   country? Agree Disgree
2. Young people are inspired by those that work in other countries.
   Agree Disgree
3. People who work in other countries never return to live in their
   homeland. Agree Disgree

Brain Drain

The exodus of educated professionals from one country to another in search of a better standard of living and access to advanced technology is known as brain drain. In the past, low-skilled laborers from around the globe supported industrialization. Gradually, the labor needs of the receiving nations shifted toward workers with advanced skills. Since that time, many immigrants have made similar journeys.

As industrialization advanced, demand for white-collar workers was partially met by specialists from other countries. In the mid-1940s, Western Europe saw its scientific elite and other experts relocating to the United States. They were attracted by higher salaries and more advanced facilities. Since 1970, the need for information technology (IT) specialists has increased tenfold as Silicon Valley became the global hub. In the last decade, the demand for healthcare workers has increased by approximately 60% worldwide. Currently, healthcare workers and IT specialists from Asia are the most prominent subjects of brain drain. This remains persistent as demand for human capital continues in developed countries.

While developed countries fill the gap with immigrants, home countries experience consequences. They invest considerable time and money in education, and the departure of those holding advanced degrees often causes a shortage of skilled labor. In addition, the loss of tax revenue slows economic growth and increases inequities between nations. As a result, funds for research and development are insufficient; hence countries cannot achieve comparable technological and scientific achievements. Nevertheless, there are also positive effects of brain drain. For example, financial remittances contribute significantly to the GDP of home countries.

As per the International Organization for Migration (IOM), $121 billion was received in remittances in 2000 and $714 billion in 2019. Which is 20 times higher than the amount in 1980 ($37 billion). Additionally, due to global communication, foreign-born workers are no longer isolated from their hometowns. Consequently, innovations multiply as migrants create professional networks with entrepreneurs in their country of origin. This circular flow of information is defined as brain circulation.

Brain drain will continue to be a reality, but not without a human cost. Professionals making the journey abroad leave behind their country, culture, customs, family, and friends. Nonetheless, one person's hopes and dreams for a better standard of living are another person's inspiration. Those left behind aspire to achieve higher levels of education to make their dreams a reality.

If you want to live a happy life, tie it to a goal not to people or things.

Albert Einstein

Brain Drain 2

Vocabulary List. （辞書必要、必ず辞書を参照してください）

No.	Word	Definition	Definition in my language	Synonyms
1	exodus (n.)			departure
2	supplement (v.)			add, supply, support
3	contributor (n.)			donor, giver, supported
4	industrialization (n.)			manufacture
5	generate (v.)			increase, produce
6	capital (n.)			asset, wealth
7	constant (adj.)			consistent, nonstop, persistent
8	inequity (n.)			unfairness
9	remittance (n.)			deposit (in the form of money)
10	isolate (v.)			separate

Definition

a. money, property, etc., that a person or business owns
b. to produce something or cause something to be produced
c. someone who gives something to help a person, group, cause or organization
d. to keep someone or something in a place or situation that is separate from others
e. many people leave a place at the same time
f. funds transferred from migrants to their home countries
g. to build and operate factories and businesses in a city, region, or country
h. something that is unfair
i. staying the same; not changing
j. something that is added to something else to make it complete

Vocabulary Review

Fill in the blanks with the words from the box below. Change the form of the words if necessary.

1. exodus	2. supplement	3. contributor	4. industrialization
5. generate	6. capital	7. constant	8. inequity
9. remittance	10. isolate		

1. Large corporations have large amounts of _____ invested into their businesses.

2. There was a(n) _____ in Ireland due to the Great Potato Famine.

3. Several _____ of the Japan Times reporters are foreigners.

4. Financial _____ occurs within countries and between countries.

5. Some families depend on financial _____ to meet their basic needs.

6. COVID-19 remains a(n) _____ concern for people all over the world.

7. Facebook _____ income from selling social media advertisements.

8. Many people _____ their income by having a part-time job.

9. The skyline of Tokyo completely changed during _____.

10. Many older people feel _____ from the rest of the world.

Idioms about *Brain Drain*

Idioms	Meaning
a brain box	a very intelligent person
a brain trust	a group of people with special knowledge who gives advice to authority
brain labor	to think hard, to make effort mentally

Please choose the correct idioms from above.

1. Indian engineers build a sustainable _____ in the America for emerging technology area.

2. We don't need to be a _____ to realize we are all equal in front of nature.

3. Mathematics makes the _____, but the reward is rich.

Check your Understanding

Answer the following questions about the reading passage.

1. What is brain circulation?
   (a) When blood flows from your brain, to your feet, and back to your brain
   (b) When you exercise your neck in a circular motion
   (c) A circular flow of information between countries

2. When did the brain drain likely begin?
   (a) After industrialization
   (b) Before industrialization
   (c) In 1980

3. Where do most IT specialists find employment in the US?
   (a) New York City
   (b) Las Vegas
   (c) Silicon Valley

4. Why are financial remittances so important to home countries?
   (a) New companies cannot be built in the home country without them
   (b) They contribute significantly to the GDP
   (c) They are used to pay off the country's debts

5. Who are the biggest contributors to the brain drain today?
   (a) Engineers, marketing managers, and pilots
   (b) IT specialists and healthcare workers
   (c) Professors and scientists

Writing about the Article

Answer each question based on the reading passage.

1. In this lesson, what is the meaning of "human capital"?

2. What job has increased tenfold in the Silicon Valley (in the US)?

3. Why have innovative advancements multiplied in home countries recently?

Interesting facts (Brain Drain)

1. Google's C.E.O., India's Sundar Pichai, came to the United States to attend Stanford on a student visa. He is now a US citizen.

2. Germany lost one of the world's greatest minds, Albert Einstein, to the United States because of the brain drain.

3. According to the World Bank, financial remittances accounted for 37.6% of Tonga's gross domestic product (GDP) in 2019.

Note

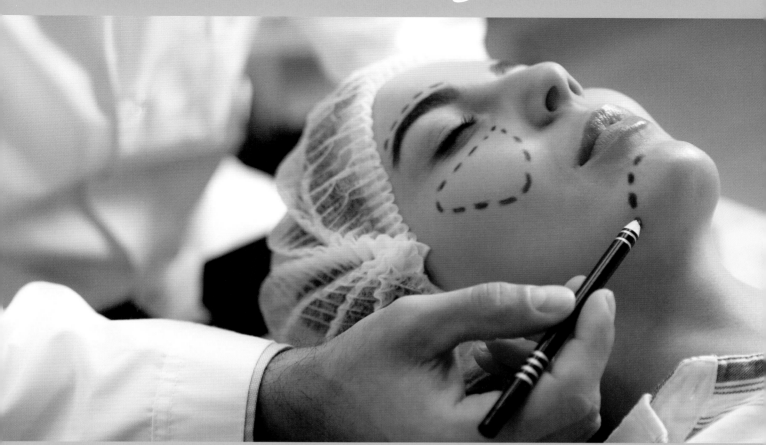

Pre-Reading questions | Discuss these questions in pairs.

1. What is cosmetic tourism?

2. What are some of the risks involved?

3. Why is cosmetic tourism increasingly popular?

What are your thoughts? | 考えましょう

1. Cosmetic surgery is worth the cost.

   Agree   Disgree

2. It's better to travel to a different country and pay less

   Agree   Disgree

3. The professional benefits outweigh the personal risks.

   Agree   Disgree

Cosmetic Tourism

Medical treatment typically used to be a local affair. Now, it is a systematically globalized business. Since 4,000 B.C.E., aesthetic journeys have been made to therapeutic, mineral-rich hot springs known for their health benefits. In ancient times, health spas sprang up in Switzerland, Greece, India and Rome. Maintaining a healthy lifestyle and youthful appearance remain just as important today as they were 6,000 years ago.

The healing waters of the past were the predecessors of future cosmetic tourism. Cosmetic tourism combines medical procedures with a vacation in an attractive destination such as Mexico or Thailand. Why do people spend so much time and money trying to look their best? Research indicates that being attractive has its perks. Attractive people are more likely to be hired for a job. Good looks are also associated with positive characteristics such as trustworthiness, intelligence, prosperity, and authority.

Economic incentives thus make people flock to foreign countries for cosmetic procedures. Breast augmentation, rhinoplasty, and eyelid surgery can cost 50%-70% less than in their home countries. According to the International Society of Aesthetic Plastic Surgery, over 27 million people traveled abroad for cosmetic operations in 2016—86.2% of whom were women. The Organization for Economic Cooperation and Development (OECD 2021) forecasted an annual increase of 25% in the next ten years.

While medical procedures can be far less expensive abroad, there are some downsides. Most insurance companies will not cover cross-border operations, forcing travelers to pay out-of-pocket. Post-operative care can be poor and can lead to infections and even death. In some cases, patients experience medical malpractice that leaves them permanently disfigured or needing corrective surgery.

Despite these pitfalls, foreign markets are benefiting in cosmetic tourism. New cosmetic surgery centers are popping up worldwide, and insurance carriers are offering cross-border health plans. India offers a medical visa (MED Visa) for medical procedures with travel insurance. Bookimed is a medical tourism agency that pairs patients with all-inclusive packages for medical care overseas. Such developments should make foreign medical treatments more appealing. After all, cultural knowledge and language skills are needed to secure international customer satisfaction. These factors are often neglected by cosmetic tourism providers. When the fulfillment of these requirements can be promised and delivered, it will enhance the business of a nation.

Cosmetic surgery can make you look beautiful; not make you feel beautiful.

Anonymous

Vocabulary List. （辞書必要、必ず辞書を参照してください）

No.	Word	Definition	Definition in my language	Synonyms
1	systematically (adv.)			carefully
2	therapeutic (adj.)			medicinal
3	mineral-rich (adj.)			natural resources
4	incentive (n.)			favor, motivation
5	augmentation (n.)			expansion, increase
6	aesthetic (adj.)			attractive, lovely
7	post-operative (adj.)			checkup, treatment
8	infection (n.)			disability, disorder
9	popping up (v.)			arriving, coming
10	provision (n.)			arrangement

Definition

a. attack or growth of germs in the body
b. expanding in amount, value, size
c. relating to the period/process following a surgery/operation
d. to appear without warning
e. having a positive effect on the body or mind
f. the act of providing, or making previous preparation
g. makes someone want to do something or work harder
h. containing a lot of minerals/naturally occurring rich substances
i. in an organized manner
j. concerned with beauty, artistic impact, or appearance

Vocabulary Review

Fill in the blanks with the words from the box below. Change the form of the words if necessary.

1. systematically	2. therapeutic	3. mineral-rich	4. incentive
5. augmentation	6. aesthetic	7. post-operative	8. infection
9. popping up	10. provision		

1. Kent teaches mathematics _____ and thoroughly.

2. Buying Hokkaido _____ mountains are one of the new sources of Investment.

3. Once again, people realized yoga as a _____ tool for healing.

4. Knowledge _____ is a continuous process for humankind.

5. Bonus payment is an emotional _____ to get work done.

6. Doctors are trying to trace the source of _____.

7. The _____ of saving is also required for future and early retirements.

8. A _____ stay is essential after significant surgery to monitor a patient.

9. Please select the option you prefer from the _____.

10. Would you mind giving me your _____ opinion for my necktie?

Idioms about *Cosmetic Tourism*

Idioms	Meaning
look like a million dollars	You look wonderful
all skin and bone	very thin or unattractive and unhealthy
be dressed to kill	wearing very fancy or attractive cloths, very well dressed up

Please choose the correct idioms from above.

1. Always being _____, makes her everyone's heartthrob.

2. When you are self-confident, you _____.

3. She is _____ after her illness.

Interesting facts (Cosmetic Tourism)

1. "Plastic" in plastic surgery is derived from the Greek word *plastikos*, which means "to form or mold."

2. The first plastic surgery procedures recorded in history date back to ancient India.

3. In Latin America, finding a plastic surgeon is as easy as finding a hairdresser.

Check your Understanding

Answer the following questions about the reading passage.

1. What is the main idea?
   (a) Traveling for cosmetic enhancement
   (b) Traveling for meditation and enlightenment
   (c) Traveling to tropical beaches

2. When did the practice of aesthetic journeys first begin?
   (a) In the spring of 2020
   (b) 1,000 years ago
   (c) In 4,000 B.C.E.

3. Where do people often travel for cosmetic procedures?
   (a) Myanmar
   (b) Thailand, Mexico and India
   (c) Kamakura

4. Why do people travel for cosmetic surgery?
   (a) To improve their physical appearance
   (b) To enjoy exotic food
   (c) To get promotions at work

5. Who is most likely to travel for cosmetic surgery?
   (a) Married couples
   (b) People over 50
   (c) Women

Writing about the Article

Answer each question based on the reading passage.

1. What is the meaning of "soft skills?"

2. How are insurance companies changing their policies to attract more travelers?

3. Why is it advantageous to look attractive?

Cosmetic Tourism

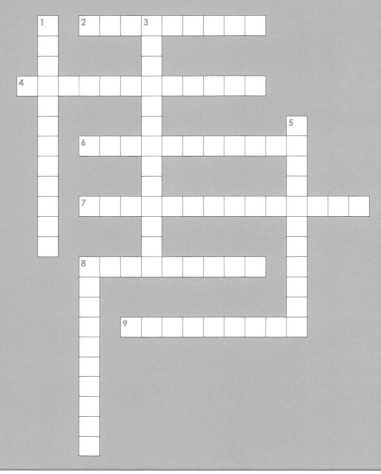

Across

2 New cosmetic surgery centers are _____ worldwide.

4 Abroad, Surgeries like breast _____ and rhinoplasty can cost 50%-70% less.

6 _____ hot springs were known for their health benefits.

7 Medical treatment is a _____ globalized business.

8 Economic _____ prompts people to flock to foreign countries.

9 The healing waters of the past prefigure the _____ journeys of future.

Down

1 Fulfillment of soft skill _____ can enhance a nation's soft power.

3 India offers travel insurance to cover the cost of _____ care.

5 Since 4,000 B.C.E., aesthetic journeys have been made to _____ hot springs.

8 Travel insurance (offered by India) helps to deal with post-operative _____.

WORD LIST

AESTHETIC   INFECTIONS   POSTOPERATIVE   THERAPEUTIC   AUGMENTATION

MINERALRICH   REQUIREMENTS   INCENTIVE   POPPINGUP   SYSTEMATICALLY

Pre-Reading questions | Discuss these questions in pairs.

1. What has changed about breakfast in modern times?
2. Which breakfast foods are most common in many countries?
3. How is breakfast important?

What are your thoughts?	考えましょう

1. Breakfast is essential for a productive day.

   Agree   Disgree

2. A big breakfast is necessary.

   Agree   Disgree

3. Skipping breakfast can have serious consequences.

   Agree   Disgree

Changing Breakfasts

In general, everyone wants to start their day "right," usually with something familiar, whatever that may be. According to one English traveler to the USA in the 1820s, most 19th-century citizens enjoyed astonishingly heavy breakfasts. In addition to tea, coffee, cold ham, and beef, "hot fish, sausages, beefsteaks, broiled fowls, fried and stewed oysters, and preserved fruits" were also common. Such a substantial start to the day may have been suitable in the past when most people spent their days plowing fields. Such rich food before running to a desk job can lead to "the great American stomachache."

Over the last century, human eating habits have changed dramatically and for the better. The ways we shop, cook, and eat have been optimized and monitored to align with our new knowledge and life goals. After the Industrial Revolution, people moved from farms to factories and offices, where much time was spent sitting or standing in one place. The heavy breakfasts that were useful before work on the farm and would now cause upset stomachs fell out of favor.

Today, eating on the go is on the rise. Some critics say that for most of human history, grocery stores did not exist. Modern eating patterns come from advertising and multinational corporations (MNCs), insisting that people eat bacon or cereal first, every morning. Various academic research findings suggest skipping this early meal affects menstrual disorders in young women. Skipping breakfast can impact academic performance or cause psychological distress in young students, affecting their cognitive achievement. On the contrary, healthy eating habits help to maintain a body mass index (BMI) within the normal range.

Business leaders often prefer morning breakfast meetings for effective persuasion and decision-making. After all, alcohol leads to an altered mindset; most of the time, if alcohol is involved, actual business does not get done. Have you ever thought about how breakfast differs in other countries? While grains, breads, and fruit are common in many parts of the world, they are served differently according to climate and altitude. In the Indian state of Maharashtra, a typical morning meal is *kande pohe*, made with pre-soaked dry rice flakes. The flakes, roasted with chilies, onions, mustard seeds, cumin and curry leaves, absorb liquids quickly and are easily digested. In Vietnam, the most iconic and popular food is *pho* rice noodles and beef soup with aromatic herbs, lime, crunchy sprouts and spicy chilies, all cooked together in the comforting heat of the soup.

In short, an energy-fueled start makes a difference in decision-making in day-to-day life. Even when one does not have time, one can eat something small on the way to work, for instance, fruit, sandwiches, or homemade rice balls for a decent start.

All happiness depends on a leisurely breakfast.

John Gunther

Vocabulary List.　(辞書必要、必ず辞書を参照してください)

No.	Word	Definition	Definition in my language	Synonyms
1	**substantial (adj.)**			**large, massive**
2	**optimize (v.)**			**develop, enhance**
3	**monitor (v.)**			**observe**
4	**gynecological (adj.)**			**menstrual, reproductive**
5	**adversely (adv.)**			**affecting, impact**
6	**cognitive (adj.)**			**intellectual**
7	**persuade (v.)**			**influence**
8	**loaf (n.)**			**bread**
9	**absorb (v.)**			**fill, occupy**
10	**iconic (adj.)**			**relating, well established, widely recognized**

Definition

a. representing something

b. acting against; working in an opposing direction

c. to do something, as by advising or urging

d. a portion of bread or cake baked in a mass

e. to take in and hold something (a liquid)

f. relating to the part of mental functions that deals with logic

g. to watch over/observing something

h. to make the best or most effective use of (a situation or resource)

i. relating to the functions and diseases specific to women and girls, especially those affecting the reproductive system

j. most important essential large, ample

Vocabulary Review

Fill in the blanks with the words from the box below. Change the form of the words if necessary.

1. substantial	2. doctor	3. monitor	4. gynecological
5. adversely	6. cognitive	7. persuade	8. loafing
9. absorb	10. iconic		

1. The smartphone helped Steve jobs to achieve _____ status.

2. The house is made of a material that _____ sound.

3. How did you _____ your parents for your Las Vegas Trip?

4. Poor lifestyle cause _____ problems in beauty.

5. During the exam, surveillance cameras were used to _____ the students.

6. India has a _____ workforce to become a global power in the 21st century.

7. The purpose of the final exam is to test students' _____ skills.

8. He spent most of the holiday just _____ around the house and garden.

9. When medicine _____ affects your health, you should stop taking it immediately.

10. Alex was under _____ supervision and could not return to work.

Idioms about *Changing Breakfasts*

Idioms	Meaning
bring home the bacon	to earn a salary, earn a living
a dog's breakfast	something or someone that looks extremely untidy, or something that is very badly done
wake up and smell the coffee	to become aware of reality, no matter how unpleasant

Please choose the correct idioms from above.

1. Michael has made a complete _____ of the research work.

2. Rose must work hard in order to _____.

3. After practising law for four years, she finally _____ that it was too much trouble for too less gains.

Check your Understanding

Answer the following questions about the reading passage.

1. What did people often eat for breakfast in the 19th century
   (a) Bacon and eggs
   (b) Steak tartare
   (c) Tea, coffee, cold ham, and beef, hot fish, sausages, beefsteaks, broiled fowls, fried and stewed oysters, and preserved fruits

2. When did eating habits begin to change?
   (a) In 1850
   (b) Over the last century
   (c) In 1998

3. Where do people often eat "kande pohe" for breakfast?
   (a) In the Western Indian State of Maharashtra
   (b) In Vietnam
   (c) In New York City

4. Why did breakfasts change dramatically?
   (a) People couldn't afford that much food
   (b) Dining room tables got smaller
   (c) Labor moved from fields to offices

5. Who needs to eat breakfast?
   (a) Athletes
   (b) Children
   (c) Everyone

Writing about the Article

Answer each question based on the reading passage.

1. In this lesson, what is the meaning of "the great American stomachache?"

2. How did the Industrial Revolution affect breakfast habits?

3. Why is breakfast important?

Interesting facts (Changing Breakfasts)

1. The ancient Romans did not believe in breakfast, only eating one meal a day at noon.
2. Eating breakfast only became a norm for all social classes in the 17th century.
3. In the 19th century, the typical UK aristocrat would have up to 24 dishes for breakfast alone.
4. Research has shown that people who skip breakfast generally have higher BMI's.

Note

Pre-Reading questions | Discuss these questions in pairs.

1. What has not changed about match making over time?
2. Which changes have made finding romance more challenging?
3. What solutions are possible if you face rejection?

What are your thoughts? | 考えましょう

1. Online dating is the only way to find a partner these days.

   Agree   Disgree

2. Social status is important for finding the right partner.

   Agree   Disgree

3. If you face rejection, you shouldn't give up.

   Agree   Disgree

Modern Love

Whenever humans interact romantically, the modern media want to nose in. Until recently, romantic matches were established through parents, priests, friends, or professional matchmakers. These intermediaries would match couples based on their characteristics or personal assumption. The attraction of the partners was based on their social status or physical attractiveness. From there, a bond was created, which could later grow into a healthy romance or even true marriage.

Today, however, internet technology has given rise to new ways to interact. With such developments, paternal institutions are being broken down as well. As modernity and gender equality have advanced, people have begun to take ownership of their own lives. Now, the multiple options available for finding a partner present a certain magic charm. One can find happiness in any part of the world. Dating apps have taken the global stage by storm: the dating app industry has been valued at over 7 billion dollars per year. These apps match people with compatible personality characteristics. Dr. Dyrenforth asked 20,000 people about their relationships and personalities. Couples with similar mindsets were indeed happier and more successful than those with dissimilar mindsets. Are dating apps then the future of love or just money-making mechanisms?

Our environment has made physical interaction a luxury since the modern work ethic has turned people into workaholics. With this, substantial interactions have been reduced. Further, match-making sites got a boom. People with poor social skills tend to experience more stress and loneliness and prefer to use these services. Finding a perfect match is always challenging on dating sites. Sudden disappearances, silence, ghosting and failure to respond to texts or emails are widespread. Overdependence on these sites may result in disappointment.

The basics of finding a partner have not changed with time or digital tools. First, the best way to meet the perfect partner is to be excited and be oneself. Do things that one is passionate about and are appealing and personally enriching. This puts you in a position to meet a significant other with similar interests, opening the door to conversation. Second, let friends know that you are available. Accept all invitations to parties, engage in group activities that you like most, or go hiking, biking, or horse riding.

Finally, nothing pulls us down like the feeling of being rejected. Indeed, we must look at rejection as a stepping stone to successful relationships. Nevertheless, when rejection happens, anyone feels spiteful about it. This forceful energy can work as a fuel for you to become so successful that the one who has denied your love will regret the loss.

It is easy to fall in love. The hard part is finding someone to catch you.

Bertrand Russell

Vocabulary List.　(辞書必要、必ず辞書を参照してください)

No.	Word	Definition	Definition in my language	Synonyms
1	matchmaker (n.)			cupids, peacemakers
2	assumption (n.)			belief, guess, if
3	dedicated (adj.)			devoted, loyal, true
4	storm (n.)			natural disaster, violent outbreak
5	substantial (adj.)			ample, large, significant
6	boom (n.)			bright, glowing, healthy
7	appealing (adj.)			attractive, charm, fascinate
8	enrich (v.)			help, upgrade
9	stepping-stone (n.)			doing progress to next level
10	spiteful (adj.)			displaying anger, harm

Definition

a. something used as a way to progress in life in critical situation

b. to be attractive

c. large in size, quantity, or value, vast

d. someone who finds suitable, dates or marriage partners for other people

e. adds value, either monetary, intellectual, or emotional

f. something increasing or developing very quickly

g. used or intended for a particular purpose

h. to move something in a very forceful and noisy way

i. the act of taking for granted, or supposing without proof

j. someone who purposely does harm to another

Vocabulary Review

Fill in the blanks with the words from the box below. Change the form of the words if necessary.

1. matchmaker	2. assumption	3. dedicated	4. storm
5. substantial	6. bloom	7. appealing	8. enrich
9. stepping-stone	10. spiteful		

1. We should read a newspaper regularly to _____ our language skill and knowledge.

2. Kenny's music _____ to young people.

3. Viki is an impressive professional _____ in the corporate world.

4. People often jump into _____ without evidence.

5. _____ words are like a bullet in a gun that are often harmful and dangerous.

6. This book is _____ to my parents and family.

7. He was _____ with good health and happiness.

8. Owning a _____ amount of money and enjoying prosperous life are two different things.

9. Annie saw this entry-level job as a _____ to a prosperous, rewarding career.

10. Keep yourself calm in a hard times, and the _____ will have moved on.

Idioms about *Modern Love*

Idioms	Meaning
love is blind	not to see the faults of the people they love
follow your heart	to act according to one's feelings
my better half	husband, wife, partner, spouse

Please choose the correct idioms from above.

1. Anne was so confused, that she decided to _____.

2. _____- he just can't see that the girl he is dating with is two timing!

3. Mrs. James has invited her friends to her party with _____.

Interesting facts (Modern Love)

1. Before it became the video sharing giant today, YouTube began as a dating site.

2. Men are usually the first ones to say "I Love you."

3. It only takes seconds to decide another person's attractiveness.

Check your Understanding

Answer the following questions about the reading passage.

1. What is the main idea?
   (a) Online dating helps people overcome the modern challenges of finding partners
   (b) Socially awkward people must use online dating to find partners
   (c) People should avoid online dating to avoid rejection

2. When did the basic principles of finding partners change?
   (a) When people became workaholics
   (b) They haven't changed over time
   (c) When people started ghosting each other

3. Where are you likely to find suitable partners?
   (a) At work
   (b) At the supermarket
   (c) Doing activities that you enjoy doing the most

4. Why has dating become more difficult?
   (a) People spend more time at work
   (b) People aren't as attractive as they used to be
   (c) Matchmakers have given up

5. Who used to help bring couples together?
   (a) Bartenders
   (b) Bosses
   (c) Parents, priests, friends, and professional matchmakers

Writing about the Article

Answer each question based on the reading passage.

1. In this lesson, what is the meaning of "similar mindsets"?

2. How has gender equality affected dating?

3. Why has dating changed so much in modern times?

Modern Love

Across

2 The Apps match people with _____ personality characteristics.
7 One must look at rejection as a _____ to successful relationships.
8 Do things that you find personally _____.
9 Do things that you are _____ about, that you find appealing and personally enriching.
10 Dating apps have taken the global stage by _____.

Down

1 Having substantive interactions vastly reduced, _____ of matchmaking sites has occurred.
3 Do things that you find _____.
4 When a rejection happens, one feels _____ about it.
5 _____ interactions have been vastly reduced.
6 Until recently, romances were established through parents, priests, friends, or professional _____.

WORD LIST

APPEALING   LOOMING   SPITEFUL   SUBSTANTIVE   COMPATIBLE
MATCHMAKERS   STEPPINGSTONE   ENRICHING   PASSIONATE   STORM

Pre-Reading questions | Discuss these questions in pairs.

1. What is changing for disabled people in many countries today?

2. What barriers have prevented disabled people from education and employment?

3. What solutions have made it easier for disabled people to attend school and work?

What are your thoughts?	考えましょう

1. Disabled people contribute to society in many ways.

Agree   Disagree

2. Disabled people have equal access to employment today.

Agree   Disagree

3. Companies need to provide barrier-free access.

Agree   Disagree

Special Need

People do not choose to be disabled. An estimated one billion people, approximately 15% of the world's population, live with a special need of some kind. Not all disorders are visible. In some parts of the world, people with disabilities have equal access to education, healthcare, and employment and are, therefore, able to be productive members of society. This was not always the case.

For a long time, people in Ghana regarded a child with a disability as a bad omen. Such kid was believed to be caused by parents' sins, evildoing, or witchcraft. Families visited medicine men for healing. A potion would be given for the disabled person to drink, almost always resulting in death. In Kyrgyzstan, families that did not have money to care for their unfit children had to institutionalize them. Sadly, these children were neglected and uneducated due to a lack of funding. They were tied to beds or locked in cages. They were viewed as inferior, less than humans. In extreme cases, medical experimentation was performed on them without their or their family's consent.

In 2006, the United Nations Convention on the Rights of Persons with Disabilities (CRPD) was created to improve the quality of life of people with special needs. Since that time, 181 nations have ratified the CRPD. In Ghana, the killing of such children was abolished. In Kyrgyzstan, these students are now attending public schools. Like many other CRPD countries, Kyrgyzstan is removing barriers to education and employment by building ramps and elevators. Additionally, organizations are being formed to help support disabled people in finding and sustaining employment.

The future looks brighter for these people as the value they bring to society is becoming more visible. Employers in the United States have seen an increase in production and sales by matching jobs to people with the right skills and abilities. Japan recently established its first talent agency for people with special needs, Co-Co Life Talent Division. The Paralympics, which highlight serious athletes, are now held alongside the Olympic Games. Australia's Madeline Stuart walks runways worldwide as the first professional model with Down syndrome. The contributions of people with special needs are beginning to be embraced globally, but we still have a long way to go.

Do not feel lonely; the whole universe is within you.

Arabic proverb

Vocabulary List.　(辞書必要、必ず辞書を参照してください)

No.	Word	Definition	Definition in my language	Synonyms
1	omen (n.)		前兆	fear, indicator, threat
2	sin (n.)			act of evil, crime, error
3	evildoing (n.)			bad, dirty, sinful, wrong
4	witchcraft (n.)			black arts, mojo, magic
5	potion (n.)			drink, dose, tonic
6	inferior (adj.)			bottom, low, secondary
7	consent (n.)			approval, permit
8	ratify (v.)			certified, finalize, proved
9	ramp (n.)			incline, rise, slope
10	embrace (v.)			hugging, accepting willingly or enthusiastically

Definition

a. sloping surface joining two different levels, as in "a wheelchair ramp"

b. a mixture of liquids

c. to take up especially readily or gladly

d. little or less importance, value or low in rank

e. something is against moral law, or law

f. communication with the devil, or with a familiar

g. to make officially valid

h. to express willingness, or to give permission

i. an event regarded as a portent of good or evil

j. anything causing, ruin, injury, or harmful activities

Vocabulary Review

Fill in the blanks with the words from the box below. Change the form of the words if necessary.

1. omen	2. sin	3. evil	4. witchcraft
5. potion	6. inferior	7. consent	8. ratify
9. ramp up	10. embrace		

1. The biggest _____ is to lose one's awareness.

2. In India receiving coconut & or rice is a sign of good _____.

3. Consumer laws should be submitted to the public for _____.

4. Adding eye-makeup will surely _____ the impact of your eyes.

5. Her grandmother _____ her warmly.

6. We are all aware of the _____ effects of the mobile phones on children.

7. How right is it to believe in _____ and fairies in adulthood?

8. Make up a magical _____ and you can charm.

9. When she told them of her noble intent, they readily _____.

10. Why should some beings be considered _____ to others?

Idioms about *Special Need*

Idioms	Meaning
at all cost / any cost	ready for everything
dream come true	something you really wanted has achieved
the sky is the limit	nothing is impossible

Please choose the correct idioms from above.

1. Chris was bent to win _____.

2. Publishing the paper was a _____ for him.

3. For an ambitious, hardworking person, _____.

Check your Understanding
Answer the following questions about the reading passage.

1. What is the main idea?
   (a) Disabled people can succeed in many ways when given the opportunity
   (b) Disabled people can be good athletes
   (c) Only a few countries provide opportunities for the disabled

2. When was the United Nations Convention on the Rights of Persons with Disabilities (CRPD) created?
   (a) In 1959
   (b) Last year
   (c) in 2006

3. Where are ramps and elevators provided for better access?
   (a) Only in Kyrgyzstan
   (b) In North America
   (c) In many CPRD countries

4. Why was the Convention on the Rights of Persons with Disabilities (CRPD) created?
   (a) To establish the Paralympics
   (b) To improve the quality of life of disabled people
   (c) To make it easier for disabled students to attend school

5. Who established Co-Co Life Talent Division?
   (a) Ghana
   (b) 181 countries
   (c) Japan

Writing about the Article
Answer each question based on the reading passage.

1. In this lesson, what is the meaning of "special needs?"

2. How can society create better conditions for people with special needs?

3. Why were disabled people mistreated in the past?

Interesting facts (Special Need)

1. Paralympics started as a friendly competition on the UK hospital ground in 1960.
2. Debuts of Badminton and taekwondo in Paralympics at Tokyo 2020.
3. Supporters needed to stay silent during football games as players rely on the ball's sound.

Note

Pre-Reading questions | Discuss these questions in pairs.

1. What do you know about Culinary Diplomacy?
2. What are the different uses of Food parties?
3. How do you think can food please people?

What are your thoughts?	考えましょう

1. The family that eats together, stays together.

　　　　　　　　　　　　　　　　　Agree　　Disagree

2. All conflicts can be resolved over dinner tables.

　　　　　　　　　　　　　　　　　Agree　　Disagree

3. Good meals can bring together people at odds.

　　　　　　　　　　　　　　　　　Agree　　Disagree

Culinary Diplomacy

Food diplomacy is a tool that uses food and cuisine to mend political divides, foster relationships, and break down barriers. This activity can involve everyone from heads of state to the family unit. Food is more than just sustenance; it represents a person's national identity, culture, and heritage.

5   Culinary diplomacy has been used since ancient times and continues to be used today. Ancient Greece solidified negotiations and peace treaties over wine and lunch with foreign leaders. In ancient Rome, peace was made with enemies through a shared meal. Former US president Ronald Reagan (1981-1989) served former leader of the Soviet Union, Mikhail Gorbachev (1985-1991), Russian caviar and wine from the Russian River Valley in California to offer a sign of
10   respect and honor the influence of Russian immigrants in this area. The soft power of food has been leveraged for millennia.

In the early 21st century (2002-2003), food began to be used to positively influence international perspectives through nation branding. The aim was increasing countries' cultural influence through food. Thailand, for example, began promoting its unique cuisine worldwide in hopes
15   of increasing exports, tourism, and international recognition of Thai food and culture. Since the campaign began, the number of Thai restaurants has increased from 5,500 (2001) to 15,000 (2019), and tourism has increased by 200%. Other countries have used similar nation-branding strategies, such as Japan, Malaysia, Peru, South Korea, Taiwan, and even North Korea.

While food can be used to strengthen social ties and reduce hostility, not every conflict can be
20   solved in this way. Disputes of some nations are so significant that leaders are not yet ready to negotiate a solution around the dinner table. In other cases, leaders are simply not interested in delicious food. In these scenarios, this type of diplomacy cannot work.

Overall, the use of food diplomacy is exploding across the globe as a serious tool for international relations in both the public and private sectors. Universities are beginning to
25   develop courses around the power of food, such as "Conflict Cuisine: An Introduction to War and Peace Around the Dinner Table" by Johanna Mendelson-Forman of the American University's School of International Service. Des Moines Public School tossed out the traditional parent-teacher conferences for Culture Night, when teachers and student's families bond over a shared meal from the students' home countries.

30   Whether connecting governments or citizens, the soft power of food continues to be a successful tool for breaking down barriers. It has the power to foster compassion and make friends of enemies. It goes without saying that culinary diplomacy will continue to grow as a valuable tool in international relations.

Note: In contrast to hard power, soft power is defined as "achieving desirable influence through attraction and cooperation".

Politics divide men, but a good meal unites them.   Motto of Le Club des Chefs des Chefs

Vocabulary List.　(辞書必要、必ず辞書を参照してください)

No.	Word	Definition	Definition in my language	Synonyms
1	foster (v.)			encourage, promote
2	involve (v.)			include
3	sustenance (n.)			diet, food, nutrition
4	leverage (v.)			hold, influence, support
5	recognition (n.)			acceptance, approval, reward
6	strengthen (v.)			confirm, support, sustain
7	hostility (n.)			bitterness, unkindness
8	savory (adj.)			aromatic, delicious, sharp
9	toss (v.)			bowl, exchange, pitch
10	compassion (n.)			affection, concern, love

Definition

a. to include completely

b. providing parental care to unrelated children, to cultivate & grow something

c. to grow strong or stronger

d. the showing of mercy towards others, to experience sympathy for

e. very strong feelings against somebody/something

f. something that provide support or nourishment

g. acceptance as valid or true

h. to throw or launch something in a given direction

i. salty, and or spicy, but not sweet

j. to use, to exploit, to manipulate in order to take full advantage (of something)

Vocabulary Review

Fill in the blanks with the words from the box below. Change the form of the words if necessary.

1. foster	2. involve	3. sustenance	4. leverage
5. recognition	6. strengthen	7. hostility	8. savory
9. toss	10. compassion		

1. Kent has achieved _____ and respect as a young researcher in the academic world.
2. You can do exercises to _____ your physical muscles.
3. There was open _____ between the two neighboring nations.
4. To _____ a relationship, both parties need willingness and cooperation.
5. Riya is _____ in many school activities, including debate, academic competition.
6. After natural disasters, the state government provided a bare quantity of food for daily _____.
7. They are determined to get more financial _____.
8. Our boss showed _____ for working from home to care for my old mother.
9. Professor _____ two drinks and left.
10. Asian foods are the most popular for their sweet and _____ meals worldwide.

Idioms about *Culinary Diplomacy*

Idioms	Meaning
piece of cake	something that is very easy to do
smart cookie	a clever person who has good ideas or very smart person
butter someone up	to please someone, to be very kind or friendly to someone

Please choose the correct idioms from above.

1. Betty _____ coach so that he wouldn't fire her for missing practice.
2. Tom is a _____ to influence all his friends to his advantage.
3. You can easily do it, it's a _____.

Interesting facts (Culinary Diplomacy)

1. In Japan an honored guest sits at the center of the table furthest from the door and begins eating first.
2. In Turkey, asking for more food is considered a compliment.
3. Indians eat with their hands because they believe it nourishes the mind, intellect, and spirit. Food has to be sensual and mindful. Eating with your hands gives you a connection with the food.

Check your Understanding

Answer the following questions about the reading passage.

1. What is the main idea?
   (a) Food can be used to influence people at all levels to make friends or enemies.
   (b) Food is for sustenance only
   (c) Not every conflict can be solved through culinary diplomacy

2. When did culinary diplomacy originate?
   (a) During the time of Former US president Ronald Reagan (1981-1989)
   (b) In the early 21st century (2002-2003)
   (c) It has been used since ancient times

3. How has promoting its unique cuisine worldwide helped Thailand commercially?
   (a) By increasing exports, tourism and growth in its restaurants
   (b) Only international recognition of Thai food and culture
   (c) By increasing its number of restaurants

4. Why are Universities developing courses around the power of food?
   (a) To strengthen social ties and reduce hostility
   (b) People are viewing its success
   (c) Because of its exploding effect in both the public and private sectors, globally

5. Who all can leverage the soft power of food?
   (a) Only persons in international relations
   (b) It can involve everyone from heads of state, universities, to the family unit
   (c) Only University heads and students

Writing about the Article

Answer each question based on the reading passage.

1. In this lesson, what is the meaning of "reduce hostility"?

2. How have each one of the following used the soft power of culinary diplomacy?
   In your home-

   Rome-

   Ancient Greece-

3. Why is it said that culinary diplomacy will continue to grow as a useful tool?

Culinary Diplomacy

Across

2 Food can be used to strengthen social ties and reduce _____.
5 Food represents a person's national identity, culture and _____.
6 international _____ of Thai food and culture.
8 It has the power to foster _____ through education.
9 The activity can _____ everyone from heads of state to the family unit.
10 Some leaders are simply not interested in _____ delicacies.

Down

1 Des Moines Public Schools _____ out the traditional parent-teacher conferences for Culture Night.
3 The soft power of food has been _____ for millennia.
4 Food is much more than just _____.
7 Food Diplomacy is a tool that uses food and cuisine to _____ relationships.

WORD LIST

COMPASSION	HOSTILITY	RECOGNITION	TOSSED	FOSTER
INVOLVE	SAVORY	HERITAGE	LEVERAGED	SUSTENANCE

Pre-Reading questions | Discuss these questions in pairs.

1. Why do some people seek change while others don't?

2. Who is likely to become happy (in the above two)?

3. What do you do to make sure that you keep winning again and again?

What are your thoughts?	考えましょう

1. Immigrants can make a difference to your country/nation.

   Agree   Disgree

2. There may be a better world beyond your borders.

   Agree   Disgree

3. Inherited benefits keep rolling-over.

   Agree   Disgree

2nd- and 3rd-Generation Immigrants

Frequently, immigrants reached new shores with only the clothes on their backs and hope welling in their hearts. This story of migration continues to repeat with new causes, be they economic, social, political, or environmental. During pre-World War II, elites such as scientists, philosophers, leaders and political figures migrated to save their own lives. Since then, there have been waves of mass migratory movements.

Subsequently, these non-natives work hard, struggle to settle, and flourish in a new land as guests. While bringing up their own children, they transfer to them the value of this struggle. From their homelands, migrants bring knowledge, unique work styles and innovative ideas based on patience and compromises.

This effort is reflected in 2nd-generation migrants developing these values and growing into solid personalities. Imbibing these values, they grow into successful adults. According to the Pew Research Center, second-generation Hispanic and Asian immigrants in the USA do better than their parents in terms of household income ($58,000 versus $46,000), the acquisition of higher education (36% versus 29%), and homeownership (64% versus 51%). 2nd-generation Indian and Chinese immigrants in London have done very well educationally. They have liberated themselves from restaurant service or factory work jobs. High-earning professionals such as entrepreneurs, doctors, professors and even Parliament members are typical examples of outsiders. For decades, members of the second generation have had a major impact on their nation's destiny.

In regard to 3rd-generation immigrants, there are typically fewer advancements. In general, they cannot be more or even as successful as previous generations. Since they already start from a more prosperous position. After all, struggling can never be the same as reading or hearing about it. The 3rd generation sees a natural gap between their lifestyles.

When an immigrant generation works hard, the fruits of its labor can be reaped and enjoyed by the next two generations. If these descendants want to prosper further, they must build upon their own legacy. They need to toil and nurture the gains. There is a need to predict and navigate the next 100 years.

The liberal and humanitarian world accepts immigrants and promises them prosperity. Now, it is up to migrants to leverage this offer to achieve success through hard work, focus and discipline. In conclusion, building an empire was not easy for our ancestors; maintaining and protecting it is a constant challenge for the next generations.

To live in a foreign country as an immigrant is all-time challenging. People will stone you for sure. To get bloody, hurt & cry or to collect the same (stones) and build your own empire; the choice is yours.

Abhay Joshi

Vocabulary List.　(辞書必要、必ず辞書を参照してください)

No.	Word	Definition	Definition in my language	Synonyms
1	shore (n.)			bank, beach, coast
2	flourish (v.)			abound, boom, shine
3	internalize (v.)			attribute, develop
4	imbibe (v.)			absorb
5	liberate (v.)			discharge, free, rescue, let go
6	descendent (n.)			future generation, successor
7	toil (v.)			hard work, struggle
8	affluent (adj.)			wealthy, lavish, luxuriant, prosperity
9	leverage (n.)			authority, control, weightage
10	pole-vault (n.)			sail over, rise, to achieve success

Definition

a. work extremely hard

b. the power to influence a person or situation to magnify gains

c. financially prosperous, born with a silver spoon in the mouth

d. to act of jumping or leaping over something

e. a person who is related to you and who lives after you

f. to set free, to release from slavery

g. land usually near a port

h. to grow well, to prosper or fare well

i. to take in, absorb

j. to make something internal, to incorporate it in oneself

Vocabulary Review

Fill in the blanks with the words from the box below. Change the form of the words if necessary.

1. seashore	2. flourish	3. internalize	4. imbibe
5. liberate	6. descendent	7. toil	8. affluent
9. leverage	10. pole-vault		

1. The player's skill set gave him a great deal of _____ in his team.

2. Plants will _____ in the rich deep soil.

3. When we _____ ideas, we listen, accept, and finally analyze.

4. He was a direct _____ of the Gandhi family.

5. We have chosen the _____ villa for a summer vacation in California.

6. Freedom fighters planned to march on and _____ the city.

7. Mr. Ryoga participated in the Tokyo Olympic _____ competition and won a gold medal.

8. When society becomes more _____ in wealth terms, time becomes more valuable.

9. Language skills help students _____ what they are learning for better understanding.

10. In this country, foreigners still _____ at the job with low pay and very long hours.

Idioms about 2nd- and 3rd-Generation Immigrants

Idioms	Meaning
go the extra mile	to work very hard to achieve something
blood, sweat, and tears	extremely hard work
eager beaver	a person who is very excited and ready to work very hard

Please choose the correct idioms from above.

1. Sayaka works eternally – first to arrive and last to leave.

   She is a real _____!

2. Riya's success wasn't due to fate; it was _____.

3. You can count on Annie; she is always willing to _____.

Check your Understanding

Answer the following questions about the reading passage.

1. What is the main idea?
   (a) Immigrants should book success through hard work, focus and discipline
   (b) Indian and Chinese immigrants in London have done very well educationally
   (c) Migration continues to repeat itself with new causes, like economic, social, political or environmental

2. When were fewer advancements seen in immigrants?
   (a) Frequently, when immigrants reached new shores with only the clothes on their backs
   (b) Typically, fewer advancements were seen in immigrants when it came to 3rd-generation
   (c) Fewer advancements are seen when an immigrant generation works hard

3. Where does one get affluent prospects?
   (a) In the liberal and humanitarian world that accepts immigrants
   (b) On new shores
   (c) Places like London, China

4. Why do people need to reach new shores?
   (a) They are driven by a thirst to secure a more prosperous lifestyle for future generations
   (b) To have hopes
   (c) Because they are tired of their old shores

5. Who will pole vault to success?
   (a) High-earning professionals such as entrepreneurs, doctors, professors, and even members of parliament
   (b) New generation which is situated in a prosperous setting from day one
   (c) Migrants who leverage immigration offer and work hard, with focus and discipline

Writing about the Article

Answer each question based on the reading passage.

1. In this lesson, what is the meaning of fewer advancements?

2. How is the goal different for each of the immigrant generation?
   i) **1st generation**

   ii) **2nd generation**

   iii) **3rd generation**

3. Why is there a gap (in lifestyle) between the 1st and the 3rd immigrant generation?

Interesting facts (2ⁿᵈ- and 3ʳᵈ-Generation Immigrants)

1. In 2018 China, India and Mexico were among the top countries of origin with immigrants in the USA.

2. 45% of USA immigrants live in 3 states. California (24%) Texas (11%) Florida (10%).

3. Indian Americans are among the most highly educated ethnic groups in the America. (PEW Research).

Note

Pre-Reading questions | Discuss these questions in pairs.

1. Which kind of company do you prefer more?
   Your own or someone else's?

2. What are the different ways of leading a fulfilling meaningful life?

3. How do you define personal development?

What are your thoughts? | 考えましょう

1. Staying single has many benefits.

   Agree   Disgree

2. Today, educated, unattached women have more
   freedom and opportunities.

   Agree   Disgree

3. Staying single can result in loneliness.

   Agree   Disgree

Happily Single

Choosing to live alone and unmarried is a way of life. Asian culture attaches enormous weight to the idea that families should live under one roof. Being single is still considered odd and taboo in many societies and cultures. Inarguably, the share of people who remain single has been escalating in newly industrialized countries. Being single is a brave choice in a world where adulthood is often considered equal to marriage and children.

In 17th-century New England, the state placed social and economic sanctions on unmarried individuals. As a result, even respected single women who devoted their lives to serving society were labeled spinsters, a rather hurtful term. Moreover, traditionally, unmarried men have had more freedom than unmarried women. Unattached men have been labeled bachelors and have not been rejected by society. Meanwhile, unmarried women have been labeled old maids. Society has tried to restrict them to the care giving roles of wife and mother rather than seeing them as individuals. Even in the 19th century, American society had not accepted men and women who chose to remain unattached. As of 2020, very few Hindus and Muslims live alone.

Today in the 21st century, singledom can be recognized in socially and culturally diverse countries such as the United States, and the European countries. "Single culture," labeled the *Ohitorisama* Movement, has risen in Japan. Although not everyone is affected by this shift, the community has started viewing singlehood as a diverse lifestyle. Today, educated, unattached women have more freedom and opportunities to pursue their dreams. As a result, they have better career aspirations than before.

Despite its continued stigmatization, staying single has many benefits. They are being able to explore one's individuality and personal development. This can offer time and freedom for platonic relationships. It allows one to travel alone on a whim and explore the world. Without a romantic relationship, a person can focus on health and financial well-being. On the other hand, loneliness may cast doubt on life choices. With age, single adults face increasing societal pressure to settle down. They may also struggle with a lack of intimacy and romantic attachment.

Ultimately, our society needs to accept singledom as a positive lifestyle choice. We must allow our youth to relish their singledom so that they can grow as complete individuals. Only this can lead to a developed society and then a nation.

How many people do you have in your home? Seven in Total. Four walls, me, shadow, and my soul.

Abhay Joshi

Vocabulary List. （辞書必要、必ず辞書を参照してください）

No.	Word	Definition	Definition in my language	Synonyms
1	enormous (adj.)			high, extreme
2	eccentric (adj.)			odd, freaky, weird
3	escalate (v.)			expand, build up, skyrocket
4	spinster (n.)			bachelor girl
5	confine (v.)			restrict, sanction
6	contemporary (adj.)			modern, relatively recent, today
7	aspiration (n.)			desire, intention, vision
8	stigmatization (n.)			abuse, criticism, put down
9	platonic (adj.)			ideal, friendly, intellectual
10	whim (n.)			craze, fantasy, desire

Definition

a. behaving unexpectedly or differently

b. very big or very great

c. something existing at the same time

d. sudden desire or change of mind

e. a hope or ambition of achieving something

f. to the next higher level of authority

g. to shut or keep in a limited space or area

h. relating to the mind, intellectual achievements

i. unfairly regarded by many people as being bad or having something to be ashamed of

j. a woman who has never been married

Vocabulary Review

Fill in the blanks with the words from the box below. Change the form of the words if necessary.

1. enormous	2. eccentric	3. escalate	4. spinster
5. confine	6. contemporary	7. aspiration	8. stigmatization
9. platonic	10. whim		

1. If the price of gasoline increases, the cost-of-living expenses will _____ soon.

2. She had one to choose her _____ mother or be with her husband.

3. They proved that John did it on a(n) _____ or in a panic situation.

4. To inherit the family business, she must remain a _____.

5. People easily _____ each other by their race, skin color, or ethnicity.

6. The old building is soon to be replaced by a more _____ architect.

7. They decided to live in relationship, mainly _____, but it quickly disappeared.

8. We should not _____ our reading to a particular area of interest.

9. Kent had a(n) _____ to become an astronaut from early childhood.

10. Social media plays a(n) _____ role in the 2010 Arab spring.

Idioms about *Happily Single*

Idioms	Meaning
move heaven and earth	to do everything you can
over the moon	extremely happy, delighted, to be very pleased
in seventh heaven	in a state of completer happiness

Please choose the correct idioms from above.

1. Father is _____ with finally winning parental authority of his son.

2. Father promised his son that he would _____ in order to get his parental authority.

3. When father and son spend time together, they are _____.

Interesting facts (Happily Single)

1. You have time to get in touch with yourself when you are single.

2. Being single gives you the space to think.

3. Single people can sleep in peace and quiet which is not cheap or easy.

Check your Understanding

Answer the following questions about the reading passage.

1. What has the author suggested at the end of the article?
   - (a) We need to let our youth grow as individuals by allowing them singledom
   - (b) Adulthood equals marriage and kids
   - (c) Singledom empowers one to travel alone on a whim and explore the world

2. When did society start viewing singlehood positively?
   - (a) Historically, in the 17th century
   - (b) Recently
   - (c) During the 18th-19th century

3. Who has had more freedom as compared to unmarried women?
   - (a) Unmarried men
   - (b) People in relationship
   - (c) Hindus and Muslims

4. Where is the phenomenon of voluntary singledom recognized today?
   - (a) Only in America
   - (b) In Muslim countries
   - (c) In civically and culturally diverse countries like the United States, France, Japan

5. Who can achieve singledom as a positive lifestyle choice?
   - (a) Only individuals living in the United States
   - (b) Truly independent individuals who have had enough room to relish their singledom
   - (c) Any individual

Writing about the Article

Answer each question based on the reading passage.

1. In this lesson, what is the meaning of happily single?

2. In America, how was singlehood seen/treated in the late 19th century?

3. Why does our society need to accept singledom as a positive lifestyle choice?

Happily single

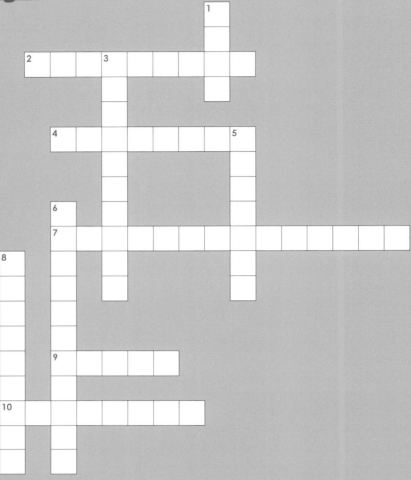

Across

2 Being single is still considered _____ and taboo.

4 Singledom can offer the time and freedom to develop meaningful _____ relationships.

7 Despite its continued _____, staying single has many benefits.

9 In many societies and cultures, being single is considered as a _____.

10 Asian culture attaches _____ weight to the idea that families should live under one roof.

Down

1 It empowers one to travel alone on a _____ and explore the world.

3 The share of singles has been _____ over the last decades.

5 Society tried to _____ women to the caring roles of wife and mother.

6 Educated women have more freedom to pursue their career _____.

8 Respected single women who devoted their lives to serving others were labeled _____.

WORD LIST

ASPIRATIONS	ENORMOUS	SPINSTERS	WHIM	CONFINE
ESCALATING	STIGMATIZATION	ECCENTRIC	PLATONIC	TABOO

Pre-Reading questions	Discuss these questions in pairs.

1. How do you differentiate between 'evolution' and 'revolution'?
2. What are some examples of 'best slaves but worst masters'?
3. What would it be like to keep your phone away, for, say a week?

What are your thoughts?	考えましょう

1. Smart phone offers us only benefits.

   Agree   Disagree

2. Smart phone/Technology challenges us in many fundamental ways.

   Agree   Disagree

3. It is not possible to choose to have disciplined browsing habits.

   Agree   Disagree

The Magic of the Smartphone

Humans are creatures that seek knowledge and information, very similarly to the way animals receive rewards from food for survival. (Indeed, the genetic difference between chimpanzees and humans is just 2%.) Humans know how to store and use this knowledge to improve the future. Smartphones are one of the best examples of this capability. Steve Jobs announced the iPhone in 2007, launching our lives 50 years ahead in the technology world.

The iPhone did not come out until six months after its initial reveal. During this time Apple turned Jobs's prototype into a mass-marketable gadget. When it finally hit stores in June, people lined up outside stores to buy one, and 270,000 phones were sold in the first two days. From there, the story of the iPhone has been one of evolution, not revolution.

Millions of people use an iPhone as their only computer, camera, GPS device, music player, means of communication, and payment tool. It puts the world in our pockets. This offers us benefits, but it certainly challenges us in many fundamental ways as well. There is endless debate on how smartphones amplify the association between modern technology and our biology. This universally accepted, everyday device has fundamentally changed us. It has been seen as harmful to concentration, sleep patterns and eyesight.

On the other hand, with the help of smartphones, scientists are trying new ways to improve the attention of children suffering from ADHD. In addition, various apps have been developed that can, for example, track one's sleep or check one's stress level, which might improve how students' brains work in the classroom. With careful consideration, we can imagine how technology can amplify opportunities to care for other human beings.

After all, whether to be the slave or the master of the smartphone is up to the individual. Therefore, what can be done to keep smartphones in their place? One can start with digital dieting, which is similar to avoiding junk food and irregular eating habits. The idea is to control the abundance of junk information and choose to have more disciplined browsing habits. One could avoid texting, say, on weekends or Friday and show one's phone who is the boss.

A Smart phone brings you closer to people far from you, but it takes you away from the ones sitting next to you.

Anonymous

Vocabulary List.　（辞書必要、必ず辞書を参照してください）

No.	Word	Definition	Definition in my language	Synonyms
1	reveal (n.)			disclosure, publication
2	evolution (n.)			development, growth
3	revolution (n.)			reform, innovation
4	fundamental (adj.)			basic, elementary, original
5	indestructible (adj.)			endless, eternal
6	significant (adj.)			amplify, impactful
7	habitual (adj.)			everyday, routine
8	abuse (n.)			harmful, hurt
9	evaluate (v.)			check, track, confirmed
10	span (n.)			duration, level, period

Definition

a. a small space or a brief portion of time

b. a leading or primary principle, rule, law, an essential part

c. to put to a wrong use, to use improperly

d. a progression of change, gradual change over time

e. to draw conclusions from examining

f. behaving in a regular manner, as a habit

g. having a noticeable or major effect, notable

h. not capable of being destroyed

i. vast change in a situation

j. to show and display that was hidden

Vocabulary Review

Fill in the blanks with the words from the box below. Change the form of the words if necessary.

1. reveal	2. evolution	3. revolution	4. fundamental
5. indestructible	6. significant	7. habitual	8. abuse
9. evaluate	10. span		

1. We should not _____ a book by its cover.

2. _____ physical activities enhance chances of being healthy.

3. Father's love is _____ towards his son.

4. People themselves become _____ due to their own thoughts.

5. The belief in hope is a(n) _____ beginning of success.

6. Limited attention _____ of the High school Japanese students is a challenge.

7. Modern _____ in technology also changes human attitude and behavior.

8. The smartphone _____ changed our lifestyle in just 20 years.

9. Life partner plays a(n) _____ role in life planning.

10. When we _____ someone's secrets, they will most likely never trust us again.

Idioms about *The Magic of the Smartphone*

Idioms	Meaning
to pull the plug	to do something that prevents an activity, prevents a plan
a well-oiled machine	something that works very efficiently or with effective coordination
work miracles	something with impressive results, to improve situation

Please choose the correct idioms from above.

1. The team has performed greatly because it plays like _____.

2. Sophie _____ with the redecoration of the house.

3. The Banks have the power _____ in the project.

Check your Understanding

Answer the following questions about the reading passage.

1. What is the main idea?
   (a) Humans are creatures that seek knowledge and information
   (b) The iPhone's story has been one of evolution, not revolution
   (c) the choice is ours: whether to become the servant or the master of a smartphone

2. Who put our lives 50 years ahead in the technology world by announcing the iPhone?
   (a) Einstein
   (b) Bill Gates
   (c) Steve Jobs

3. Why did iPhone not come out until six months after its initial reveal?
   (a) People weren't happy with this reveal
   (b) This time was used to turn Steve Jobs's prototype into a mass-marketable gadget
   (c) This time was used by Apple for promotion

4. How many phones were sold in the first two days (When it finally hit stores)?
   (a) 30,000
   (b) When it finally hit stores, 270,000 phones were sold in the first two days
   (c) Few

5. What can the phone apps achieve?
   (a) Track one's sleep or check one's stress level, improve how students' brains work
   (b) Both (a) & (c)
   (c) Improve the attention of children suffering from ADHD

Writing about the Article

Answer each question based on the reading passage.

1. What do smart phones symbolize?

2. Complete the following analogy / co-relation:
   Humans:

   Animals:

3. Why is it said that a smartphone puts the world in our pockets?

Interesting facts (The Magic of the Smartphone)

1. 49% of the world population on earth owned a smartphone device in 2021.

2. The first mobile device was sold in the America in 1983 for $4,000.

3. On an average, a person unlocks the phone 4 times in an hour, around 110 times each day in total.

Note

Pre-Reading questions   Discuss these questions in pairs.

1. What do you do only for pure enjoyment?
2. How often do you hear these words around you: stress, anxiety, trauma?
3. What would it feel like if you call yourself and no one picks up?

What are your thoughts?	考えましょう

1. The people you love are the ones to get you through your tough times.   Agree   Disgree
2. When we are completely involved in something we enjoy it most.   Agree   Disgree
3. Having more of material things brings more of happiness.   Agree   Disgree

Mindfulness

Mindfulness is the fundamental human strength of "paying attention, on purpose, in the present moment, without judging." It helps us realize and enhance the best part of ourselves as human beings. It is a practice involved in various religious and secular traditions from Hinduism and Buddhism and, more recently, nonreligious meditations. Some argue that the history of mindfulness is also rooted in Judaism, Christianity and Islam.

In the 1970s, Jon Kabat-Zinn founded the Center for Mindfulness at the University of Massachusetts Medical School. He made it known to the world. Some people are always physically or mentally busy. In addition, technology leads us to want to be connected and have something to do, leaving few occasions to just "be."

Multitasking has become fundamental to our generation. We often text while watching TV and look at our phone while walking on the sidewalk. Likewise, even after office hours, people often bring work home. The more we do, the more stressed we feel. For example, modern educators and students carry so much on their shoulders. Fulfilling academic and social expectations is demanding. Although our world is moving and changing faster than ever, students are facing new challenges. This affects their ability to focus, regulate emotions, build inner resilience and form healthy and supportive relationships. In developed countries, nearly 1 in 3 students experience anxiety by the age of 18. Nearly 40% of high school students feel lonely and left out. In the USA, 46% of all children have experienced trauma. There is a solution to every problem. We usually need only time, money, or personal attention to resolve it. No problem falls outside the reach of these factors. So, stay grounded to find the right solution.

Mindfulness comes in many different forms, such as yoga, Zen practice or even washing dishes. As Thich Nhat Hanh advocates paying attention to the purpose is the essential part. According to Duke University of Medical Research data, among US practitioners, an hour of yoga per week reduces stress levels. This ultimately cuts an individual's healthcare costs by an average of $2,000 yearly.

In a world of constant stress and disruption, simply sitting still and relaxing for a while is essential. It has gradually become part of the self-help movement. One should start each day with a must-do list, step away from screen at specific times and focus on one thing at a time. Stress can strike at any time, so practising meditation daily is the ultimate solution.

He said, "There are only two days in the year that nothing can be done. One is called yesterday and the other is called tomorrow, so today is the right day to love, believe, do, and live utmost."

<u>Dalai Lama</u>

Vocabulary List.　（辞書必要、必ず辞書を参照してください）

No.	Word	Definition	Definition in my language	Synonyms
1	mindfulness (n.)			attention, awarness
2	enhance (v.)			better, improves
3	multitasking (n.)			juggling
4	backpack (n.)			carry so much on their shoulders
5	resilience (n.)			courage, resolve, vim
6	anxiety (n.)			fear, tension, worry
7	trauma (n.)			pain, shock, stress
8	stay grounded (v.)			being sensible and reasonable
9	advocate (n.)			backer, booster, supporter
10	eventually (adv.)			gradually, ultimately

Definition

a. to be raised up, to grow larger

b. carrying things in a bag packed on one's back

c. a person who speaks in support of something

d. an understanding or awareness of something

e. not to develop an ego or stay normal

f. emotional shock following a stressful event or a physical injury, which may lead to long-term instability

g. a feeling of worry, nervousness, or unease about something with an uncertain outcome

h. to schedule and execute multiple program

i. in the end

j. the mental ability to handle or recover quickly from hardship

Vocabulary Review

Fill in the blanks with the words from the box below. Change the form of the words if necessary.

1. mindfulness	2. enhance	3. multitasking	4. backpack
5. resilience	6. anxiety	7. trauma	8. stay grounded
9. advocate	10. eventually		

1. Every day, bring _____ to each activity.

2. Calm mind _____ the brain's ability in a difficult situation.

3. Compared to men, women are often very good at _____.

4. Car manufacturer has a history of being _____ after a crisis in the market.

5. They will have to _____ food supplies through the hike.

6. Kent always _____ despite all the fame and praise.

7. _____, we learn to control our thoughts and cry inside.

8. Medical Doctors will _____ healthy eating for their patients.

9. Rintaro never fully recovered from the _____ he suffered during his childhood.

10. College students are _____ about money, marriage, and job hunting.

Idioms about *Mindfulness*

Idioms	Meaning
all ears	to be waiting eagerly to hear about something
all heart	to be very kind and generous
on your toes	to be alert

Please choose the correct idioms from above.

1. Kids became _____ when the teacher started telling them a story.

2. When the surgeon walked in, the entire staff was _____ to serve him.

3. Valentine's day videos don't have to be _____ and flowers.

Interesting facts (Mindfulness)

1. Mindfullness is not religious.

2. Mindfullness prepares you to have self-control in tough situations.

3. If you never try mindfulness, you will never know the happiness in it.

Check your Understanding

Answer the following questions about the reading passage.

1. What is the core benefit of mindfulness?
   - (a) It helps us realize and enhance the best part of ourselves as human beings
   - (b) It makes us multitask
   - (c) It helps us to complete must-do list

2. Who brought the practice of mindfulness to prominence around the globe?
   - (a) Duke university of Medical Research data
   - (b) Jon Kabat-Zinn brought the practice of mindfulness to prominence around the globe
   - (c) Thich Nhat Hanh advocated and popularised mindfulness globally

3. What is multi - tasking?
   - (a) Doing 2-3 or more tasks at a time
   - (b) Multitasking means facing new challenges
   - (c) It is a part of our generation

4. What affects the ability to focus attention and regulate emotions?
   - (a) Changes
   - (b) Stress
   - (c) Challenges

5. How can stress levels be reduced?
   - (a) Multitasking
   - (b) Keeping very high expectations
   - (c) An hour of yoga per week can reduce stress levels radically

Writing about the Article

Answer each question based on the reading passage.

1. In this lesson, what is the meaning of mindfulness?

2. Mindfulness comes in many different forms like:

3. What does Thich Nhat Hanh advocate?

Mindfulness

Across

1 This affects their ability to build inner _____.

6 _____ has become part of our generation.

8 It helps us realize and _____ the best part of ourselves as human beings.

9 In developed countries, nearly 1 in 3 students faces _____ by the age of 18.

Down

1 To _____ a problem, we need time, money, and personal attention.

2 _____ with those who are important to you.

3 _____ is a fundamental human strength.

4 As Thich Nhat Hanh _____ paying attention to the purpose is essential.

5 An hour of yoga per week reduces stress, _____ cutting annual healthcare costs by an average of $2,000.

7 In America, 46% of all children have experienced childhood _____.

WORD LIST

ADVOCATES	MINDFULNESS	RESOLVE	ULTIMATELY	ANXIETY
MULTITASKING	STAYGROUNDED	ENHANCES	RESILIENCE	TRAUMA

Pre-Reading questions **Discuss these questions in pairs.**

1. What is your dream partnership?
2. What, according to you, is a successful marriage?
3. Why should 'marriage' as an institution exist and flourish?

What are your thoughts?	考えましょう

1. Equality in a marriage brings strength to it.

   Agree   Disgree

2. Perfect marriage is the foundation of a strong nation.

   Agree   Disgree

3. Learning to love oneself completely is the key
   to a successful partnership.

   Agree   Disgree

Marriage

Society comes before individuals, so humans must satisfy specific basic needs to survive. As he became a rational social being, coupling and living together as a community became even more vital. Therefore, the arrangement of marriage is an enhancement of trust between two individuals. Today, individuals marry for emotional, libidinal, financial, and religious purposes. This knot, which some believe is tied in heaven, often frays, and its permanence is continually threatened. Nevertheless, the bond of marriage has embodied the benefit of partnership and ideal stability.

Historically, for economic reasons, a gendered division of labor was implemented. Consequently, men started earning money and obtaining property. So, women became responsible for the domestic tasks of childcare and raising families. With the rise of patriarchy, womenfolk suffered denial. Their labor and skills were undervalued and seen as weak and dependent. With modernization, however, this gender bias is healing. Ironically, educated womenfolk became far more powerful. Their monetary empowerment insured them from being exploited by their male counterparts. Thus, wedlock gives them more equality and perhaps more satisfaction.

This holds true only for those male partners who can appreciate and welcome this change. It is a conflict and a loss of the "perfect" union for those who do not. With financial independence, women now have enough space to run if marriage causes them trouble. They do not want to compromise to sustain a troublesome marriage.

Today, separation rates are increasing (65%- 70% of couples in America); hence people are eager to help those undergoing such separation. Governments, too, may be supportive since they know from research that broken families stress the entire system, leading to a physically and mentally sick public. This view is even more widespread in Asia. In an interview in 1994, Lee Kuan Yew, former prime minister of Singapore, said that stable marriages make a sustainable and sound society. It means a happy family, creating a stable next generation. This stable generation is the foundation of a strong nation. He feared that collapse of the family would be the main threat to the success of Singapore.

To save the collapse, the responsibility is on both partners. They may draw support from their elders (parents and in-laws) or externally from professional counselors. There are many ways to strengthen a marriage, but the will to do so is the most basic requirement.

One could look at this issue differently: How about loving, marrying, and committing to oneself before another person? It means to love ourselves the way we want our partners to love us. After all, love blossoms through patience and tolerance, for a genuinely profound relationship of giving and taking.

Never call in a cat to settle the argument of two birds.

Indian wisdom

Vocabulary List.　(辞書必要、必ず辞書を参照してください)

No.	Word	Definition	Definition in my language	Synonyms
1	rational (adj.)			convincing, sensible, wise
2	enhancement (n.)			boost, growth, progress
3	libidinal (adj.)			passionate
4	fray (v.)			unravel, wear out
5	permanence (n.)			continuance, stability
6	embody (v.)		具現化する	describe, realize, show
7	ironically (adv.)		皮肉に	madly, unwisely, weakly
8	empowerment (n.)			approval, authorization
9	wedlock (n.)			bridal knot, marriage
10	profound (adj.)			deep, emotional, thoughtful

Definition

a. being very different from what you would usually expect

b. something which has been proven to be real, continued survival

c. likely to be understood by intellectuals, deep

d. the state of being married

e. the act of improving quality

f. the granting of political, social, or economic power to an individual or group

g. able to think sensibly or logically

h. to represent a quality or an idea exactly

i. threads coming loose at the edge

j. a feeling of strong desire

Vocabulary Review

Fill in the blanks with the words from the box below. Change the form of the words if necessary.

1. rational	2. enhancement	3. libido	4. fray
5. permanence	6. embody	7. ironically	8. empowerment
9. wedlock	10. profound		

1. Do you know the _____ Indian Nobel prize winner?

2. After five long years, finally, the loving twosome are now in _____.

3. A lot of work is done these days for women's _____.

4. These days _____ of job is becoming rare.

5. _____, the champion lost to an amateur.

6. Prof. Sawa _____ the best qualities of a teacher.

7. The dress is _____ at its seams.

8. Stress and anxiety are the main causes affecting the _____.

9. The Chef _____ the flavor of the dish by using Japanese pepper. (*sansho*)

10. Meghana is a(n) _____ and elegant woman.

Idioms about *Marriage*

Idioms	Meaning
apple of my eye	they are very important to you; one is extremely fond & proud
tie the knot	get married
blind date	a meeting between two person who never meet before

Please choose the correct idioms from above.

1. My child is the _____.

2. If you think you are perfect for each other, why don't you _____ soon?

3. She agreed to go on the _____ because it was set up by her well-wishers.

Check your Understanding

Answer the following questions about the reading passage.

1. What are the various reasons for marrying?
   (a) Tradition must be followed
   (b) Social, emotional, libidinal, financial, legal, political, spiritual and religious
   (c) Whim, fancy

2. When did Lee Kuan Yew say that perfect marriage makes a sound society?
   (a) Historically
   (b) In the 1830s
   (c) In an interview in 1994

3. Where is the view held very widely that broken families stress the entire system?
   (a) This view is held very widely globally
   (b) Only in Singapore
   (c) This view is held very widely in Asia

4. Why do women now have enough space to run if marriage causes them trouble?
   (a) Because they have domestic responsibilities
   (b) Women are independent, well-supported and don't need to suffer a troublesome marriage
   (c) Because gender bias is healing

5. Who is/are to keep the wedlock firm and strong?
   (a) Professional counselors, social forums, and media
   (b) Both, husband and wife
   (c) Elders in family - parents and in-laws

Writing about the Article

Answer each question based on the reading passage.

1. Complete the following:
   Perfect marriage → happy family → stable next generation → _____

2. How has the onus of "keeping the marriage strong" shifted over time?
   Historically -
   with modernization -
   currently -

3. What does "Loving" mean, in this lesson?

Interesting facts (Marriage)

1. Female breadwinner couples have a considerably higher risk of divorce than male breadwinner couples.
2. 75% of people who marry partners from an affair eventually divorce.
3. Couples who pleased each other often are more likely to stay together.

Note

Pre-Reading questions | Discuss these questions in pairs.

1. How well versed are you in your own mother tongue?
2. What do you think of multilingualism?
3. What are the challenges in learning a new/foreign language?

What are your thoughts? | 考えましょう

1. Multilingualism is an undeniable advantage.

   Agree   Disgree

2. Learning a new language can have manifold benefits.

   Agree   Disgree

3. It is easy to pick up a new language.

   Agree   Disgree

The Power of Learning a Foreign Language

In an increasingly connected world, proficiency in a foreign language is an unquestionable asset. Even though learning an unfamiliar lexicon can be challenging, it opens up a world of possibilities and presents numerous academic, professional, and social benefits. Before World War I, regional multilingualism was a cherished skill. People worldwide are passionate about various local dialects; however, there was a massive shift in our perception of languages during and after WW II. English nativism gained political and cultural predominance in many post-colonial countries, making people lose the will to learn new vocabulary.

Nevertheless, interest in learning new languages grew from 1950 to 1990. Today, multilingualism is once again considered an undeniable advantage. The current political and social encouragement is toward diversity. This has inspired many individuals to engage with new lexicons of which they are not native speakers.

There are many benefits to learning a new language in today's highly interconnected global landscape. Mastering a second language is a gateway to exploring new cultures and international communities. It is considered a valuable skill in job applications to pursue overseas academic and work opportunities. Employers prefer to hire international applicants who are proficient in the employer's tongue. It also helps one explore untranslated literature from different global communities that would otherwise be inaccessible. It also allows people to expand their worldview and connect with unique individuals from other communities.

Moreover, there are many cognitive benefits attached. These include developing critical thinking, boosting memory, enhanced problem solving, and increased creativity and multitasking ability. Picking up a second language develops and primes new brain networks. Hence, it makes it easier for one to learn even more languages.

That said, picking up a new language is certainly not easy. It requires dedication, patience, time, and a great deal of practice. Moreover, joining a paid tutoring program that offers certification can be expensive. Despite its challenges, learning a foreign language is a beneficial life skill. It helps define one's future aim and shape one's perspective in this ever-evolving world. Ultimately, the secret to commanding a foreign language depends on how proficiently a person can speak and understand his or her mother tongue.

If you talk to a man in a language he understands, that goes to his head. If you talk to him in his own language, that goes to his heart.

Nelson Mandela

Vocabulary List.　（辞書必要、必ず辞書を参照してください）

No.	Word	Definition	Definition in my language	Synonyms
1	lexicon (n.)			dictionary, terminology
2	multilingualism (n.)			diverse, nonracial, open
3	steam (n.)			actively engaged, passionate, zeal
4	dialects (n.)			local language, vernacular
5	colloquial (adj.)			familiar, nativism
6	momentum (n.)			ambition, predominance, will power
7	versed (adj.)			expert, proficient
8	cognitive (adj.)			analytical, intellectual
9	dedication (n.)			devotion, faith, loyalty
10	endeavor (n.)			aim, efforts, goal, tasks

Definition

a. things done to achieve an aim

b. relating to one's mental functions or abilities

c. the quality of being committed to a task or purpose

d. drive or ambition in achieving one's goals

e. a regional or minority language

f. able to communicate fluently in multiple languages

g. the vocabulary of a language

h. displaying outstanding skill, knowledge, or experience in a given field

i. energy or force that drives activity or action

j. used in or for everyday conversation rather than formal or official contexts

Vocabulary Review

Fill in the blanks with the words from the box below. Change the form of the words if necessary.

1. lexicon	2. multilingualism	3. trait	4. inaccessible
5. asset	6. momentum	7. prime	8. cognitive
9. dedication	10. endeavor		

1. Nick was _____ well for the interview.

2. The roads are narrow, curvaceous, and _____ to lofty cars.

3. Honesty is an admirable _____.

4. His career is gaining _____ day by day.

5. A right diet can directly improve one's _____ functions.

6. Janet has several worthy _____ like looks, intelligence, character and more.

7. _____ is very common in countries like India.

8. Hard work equals success in most people's _____.

9. It was a huge _____ to get the tiny twins dressed and ready to perform on stage.

10. Michael has _____ his book to his parents.

Idioms about *The Power of Learning a Foreign Language*

Idioms	Meaning
to open up a world of	to create new opportunities
to pick up	to improve or cause to improve in condition or activity
secret to success	lesser known path to success

Please choose the correct idioms from above.

1. Serena _____ the dance steps within no time.

2. Internet _____ to the youth around the globe.

3. Kent's _____ is his creative writing skill.

Interesting facts (The Power of Learning a Foreign Language)

1. There is no official language in the US.

2. A second language skill can make you cleverer, help to slow down the aging process of the mind.

3. English has the most vocabulary of any known language with 75,000 words.

Check your Understanding

Answer the following questions about the reading passage.

1. What is the main idea?
   (a) Before colonization, regional multilingualism was a cherished trait
   (b) Proficiency in a foreign language is an unquestionable asset
   (c) It is certainly not easy to pick up a new language

2. When did the interest in learning new lexicons grow?
   (a) It has always been a cherished trait
   (b) During and after the colonial era
   (c) Interest in learning new lexicons grew in the mid- to late 1900s

3. What are the benefits of learning a foreign language?
   (a) It opens up numerous possibilities and academic, professional, and social benefits
   (b) It helps learn new vocabulary
   (c) Helps one explore foreign lands

4. What are the cognitive benefits attached to learning an unfamiliar language?
   (a) Both (b) and (c)
   (b) Critical-thinking skills, boosted memory, enhanced problem solving
   (c) Increased creativity and multitasking ability

5. How to pick up a new language?
   (a) Any tutoring program can be used
   (b) Through dedication, patience, time, money and a great deal of practice
   (c) From overseas employers

Writing about the Article

Answer each question based on the reading passage.

1. In this lesson, why does the author emphasise the importance of mother tongue?

2. In this lesson, what does each of the following mean?
   Beneficial life skill –

   An individual's gateway to new explorations –

   An unquestionable asset -

3. Why is learning a new language considered a valuable skill for professional progress?

The Power of Learning a Foreign Language

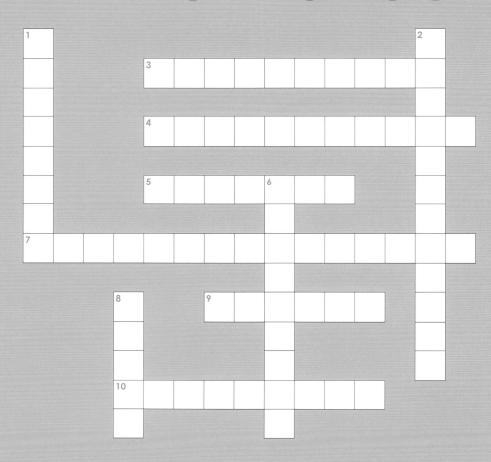

Across

3 It requires _____, patience, time, and a great deal of practice.
4 _____ in a foreign language is an asset.
5 Learning an unfamiliar _____ can be challenging.
7 Before colonization, regional _____ was a cherished trait.
9 Picking up a second language _____ new brain networks.
10 Learning a foreign language helps define one's future _____.

Down

1 The current political and social _____ is leaning toward diversity and inclusivity.
2 Learning a foreign language helps one explore untranslated literature which is _____.
6 There are many _____ benefits attached to learning a new language.
8 In an increasingly connected world, foreign language is an unquestionable _____.

WORD LIST

ASSET
INACCESSIBLE
ENDEAVORS
MULTILINGUALISM
MOMENTUM
DEDICATION
PROFICIENCY
LEXICON
COGNITIVE
PRIMES

1. How do you describe your sleep?
2. What are the various aspects to sleep?
3. What solutions do you have for sleeplessness?

What are your thoughts?	考えましょう

1. Sound sleep is a gift; it cannot be acquired through efforts.

   Agree   Disgree

2. Lack of sleep means lack of health.

   Agree   Disgree

3. Good practice of sleep ensures progress in life.

   Agree   Disgree

Sleep

The most astonishing activity a person can engage in is sleeping. It is an essential biological function that plays a vital role in the formation and enrichment of our minds. Thus, it directly affects happiness, mood, memory, and concentration. The precise reason why we sleep is still unclear, and the question remains a mystery in health science. The biological function of sleep is one of the very few scientifically proven explanations.

Sleep is the practice of closing our eyes and letting the body and brain rest and recharge for the day ahead. This may sound like a simple thing, but it is significant for the functioning of our bodies. According to the National Center for Biotechnology Information, within a minute after going to bed, noticeable changes occur in the brain and body. Our temperature and heart rate drop because our energy consumption is lower during this period. In this process, the brain cells send electrical signals and release healing chemicals. As a result, the body and brain both have time to rest for the busy day ahead.

Some say that sleep releases one's wildest thoughts and dreams. While we sleep, brain cells send electrical signals back and forth to each other. These include recent memories being converted into long-term memory through the neural path. While doing so, they collide, bump into each other, and strange images are seen in dreams.

Think of this process: Our brain is like a film director, writer, and actor all in one. How long does a human need to sleep on average to enjoy these homemade movies? The amount depends on one's age. Adults aged 18 to 60 require at least 7 hours, and those who do not get enough of it may easily suffer from symptoms such as being short-tempered and tired. Ultimately, a lack of sleep may interfere with work concentration, impoverishing a person financially and physically.

Finally, sleeping trouble is a universal problem. Try this habit: Avoid screen time at least two hours before bed and wake up at the same time to establish a routine. Even sleeping on one's stomach can help one fall asleep quicker. After all, maintaining physical, mental, and financial health is a practice. The individual is responsible for creating or destroying his or her own life. In this context, thus, sleeping plays a very meaningful role.

Sleep is an investment in the energy you need to be effective tomorrow.

Tom Roth

Sleep *14*

Vocabulary List.　(辞書必要、必ず辞書を参照してください)

No.	Word	Definition	Definition in my language	Synonyms
1	astonishing (adj.)			amazing, fantastic
2	formation (n.)			growth, shaping
3	enrichment (n.)			enhancement, progress
4	healing (adj.)			medical, therapeutic
5	neural (adj.)			cardiac, nerve
6	collide (v.)			crash, knock
7	weird (adj.)			crazy, odd, strange
8	symptom (n.)			evidence, signs
9	absolute (adj.)			entire, perfect, ultimately
10	routine (n.)			every day, frequent

Definition

a. a regular series of movements or fixed way of doing things

b. an improvement to the quality of something

c. the action of forming or process of being formed something

d. strange in nature

e. any feeling or illness pr physical or mental change that is caused by a disease

f. to push roughly

g. relating to or affecting the nerves

h. total and complete

i. giving comfort

j. inconceivable or mind-boggling

Vocabulary Review

Fill in the blanks with the words from the box below. Change the form of the words if necessary.

1. astonishing	2. formation	3. enrichment	4. impoverish
5. neural	6. collide	7. weird	8. symptom
9. treat	10. routine		

1. The course has _____ subjects like art and music.

2. Poor farming practices _____ the soil.

3. Doctor _____; God heals!

4. The two cars _____.

5. Thank God! The _____ nightmare ended soon!

6. The new _____ of coffee with her was very pleasing.

7. The _____ are too bold to be missed.

8. The new bridge was built at a(n) _____ speed.

9. Eye-pleasing _____ were the main attraction of the show.

10. _____ therapy was used to help the injured worker.

Idioms about *Sleep*

Idioms	Meaning
a catnap	a short sleep during the daytime, a short sleep, light nap
beauty sleep	the sleep-in order to feel and look healthy, potentially more beautiful
sound asleep	sleeping deeply

Please choose the correct idioms from above.

1. _____ sometimes does wonders to your moods.

2. You book your _____ while I catch up on the missed sessions.

3. My grandfather often gets _____ during a din.

Check your Understanding

Answer the following questions about the reading passage.

1. What is the role of sleep in our life?
   - (a) Sleep plays a vital role in the formation of our minds, health and life progress
   - (b) To save on our energy consumption
   - (c) Sleep allows the release of the wildest thoughts and dreams

2. What is sleep?
   - (a) It is a simple, insignificant thing we do every day
   - (b) It is something that we do to fill the time gap between two days
   - (c) Sleep is the practice of closing our eyes and letting the body and brain rest

3. How long does a human need to sleep on an average?
   - (a) Adults aged 18 to 60 require at least 7 hours of sleep on an average
   - (b) For adult humans, 4 hours is enough
   - (c) There is no such fixed time span

4. Why does our temperature and heart rate drop when we go to sleep?
   - (a) Because our brain is resting
   - (b) So that healing chemicals can be released
   - (c) Because our energy consumption lowers, and the body is to settle down and rest

5. Why does sleep play a vital role in the formation and enrichment of our minds?
   - (a) Because it is a daily routine activity
   - (b) Because it has direct effects on happiness, mood, memory, and concentration
   - (c) Because it is a mystery in health science

Writing about the Article

Answer each question based on the reading passage.

1. Less sleep results into?

2. What all happens after going to sleep?
   Our temperature

   Our brain sends

3. Why is brain like a film director, writer, lead, and videographer, all in one?

Interesting facts (Sleep)

1. Finding hard to get out of bed in the morning is a signal of depression or lack of nutrition.

2. Statistics shows that an extra hour of sleep reduces risk of traffic accidents.

3. Women are more likely to multitask and hence take longer to recover so, they sleep more than men.

Note

1. Which country/ ies do you think are leaders in Space Business?
2. How do you think is this industry helpful to common man?
3. What is Japan's role in global Space Business?

What are your thoughts?	考えましょう

1. Ambition to control space is a modern desire.

   Agree Disgree

2. The space business is a lucrative field.

   Agree Disgree

3. Space exploration has emerging problems.

   Agree Disgree

The Space Business

The "space business" is an umbrella term for space-related enterprises. This industry aims to help humans by providing communication services, navigational tools, climate forecasts, spying, and more. In the past, this business was operated by and for the armed forces. Now it is mainly done by private companies and governments of developed countries with local, highly skilled human capital. The data generated by these businesses are used for defense and commercial purposes.

Historically, humans were not able to realize their ambitions of controlling space. These aspirations had existed since 1957, when the Soviet Union launched the first artificial satellite, Sputnik, into orbit. In 1962 NASA sold space to private entities for commercial satellites to tap the promising economy full of opportunities. Nevertheless, failures were common until the 1970s, when launch technology became reliable. Things have certainly changed over the years. In 1986, after the Challenger space shuttle exploded, NASA stopped launching projects. Later, the Pentagon became a new customer of private launch firms.

Today, the interplanetary enterprise is enjoying a rise in popularity. Many private organizations worldwide, including in China, successfully launch rockets with human crews into the cosmos. Since 1993, India has launched 342 foreign satellites for 34 countries via its *Polar Satellite Launch Vehicle. India ranks fifth among all countries in the world regarding space tech businesses and is becoming a hub for small satellites. The government of India has opened this business to private players. As a result, 350 ventures are developing low-cost solutions on par with global powers.

Like their Cold War ancestors, these Asian giants have specific aims and a thirst for publicity. Japanese companies are already supplying robots and satellite tools. This type of business is undoubtedly lucrative, with global revenues nearing $385 billion. Economists expect revenues to be in the trillions of dollars by the middle of this century. This industry is creating various tech industry jobs, benefiting the world economy and human well-being.

Nevertheless, space exploration has encountered emerging problems, such as cosmic debris. Moreover, at present, we are unable to move past geopolitical rivalries. These conflicts continue to affect approaches to outer-space exploration. To resolve those issues, we need to remove geopolitical hurdles and increase the collaborative study of the cosmos. The day is not far when our children or grandchildren will tell us that they are heading out on a space excursion from school the following week.

* Polar Satellite Launch Vehicle (PSLV) 極軌道打ち上げロケット。(インドは 1963 年から独自の衛星とその打上げ手段の開発に乗り出した。インド宇宙研究機構 Indian Space Research Organization (ISRO) の開発した第 3 世代の打上げ機。)

Unless humanity gives top priority to the space science there will be no future for the humanity.

Mehmet Muran Ildan

Vocabulary List. （辞書必要、必ず辞書を参照してください）

No.	Word	Definition	Definition in my language	Synonyms
1	prediction (n.)			forecasts, speculation
2	aspiration (n.)			aim, purpose, target
3	entity (n.)			individual, organizational
4	interplanetary (adj.)			astronomic, in the sky, solar
5	surge (n.)			accelerating, expanding, rise
6	cosmos (n.)			solar system, space, universe
7	ancestor (n.)			antecedents, race
8	lucrative (adj.)			beneficial, rewarding
9	revenue (n.)			remuneration, yield
10	exploration (n.)			discovery, odyssey

Definition

a. one's family or ethnic descent

b. producing a surplus or profitable

c. the action of research in an unfamiliar area

d. a person's financial resources, income

e. increasing, especially suddenly and powerfully

f. a statement of what will happen in the future

g. a hope or ambition of achieving something

h. relating to the universe or cosmos

i. something that exists separately from something else and has its own identity

j. the whole world or the universe

Vocabulary Review

Fill in the blanks with the words from the box below. Change the form of the words if necessary.

1. ambitious	2. emphasize	3. entity	4. interplanetary
5. surge	6. cosmos	7. geopolitical	8. lucrative
9. revenue	10. exploration		

1. Alexander was a(n) _____ warrior.

2. The Institute _____ collaborative learning.

3. Peace and security are high on _____ agenda.

4. It is sad but true that crops like tobacco and opium are _____ crops.

5. The three companies are competing _____.

6. She could not contain the _____ of excitement.

7. It is expected that _____ will increase this year.

8. It would be naive to take a bright star as _____.

9. Students were asked to make a model of the _____.

10. For more information, _____ through internet has become common.

Idioms about *The Space Business*

Idioms	Meaning
umbrella term	blanket term, a term used to cover a broad category of functions
on par	on the same level or standard
living on another planet	not noticing what is happening around them or not being realistic

Please choose the correct idioms from above.

1. These days Daniel seems as if he is _____.

2. "Jacket" is quite a(n) _____ in the fashion world.

3. Her book is _____ with the best sellers.

Interesting facts (The Space Business)

1. Space is full of debris, used rocket parts and dead satellites by USA, Russia and China.

2. India has launched 342 satellites for 36 countries as of 1999 - 2021 and 250 for USA.

3. Toyohiro Akiyama is the first Japanese journalist who reported from outer space in 1990.

Check your Understanding

Answer the following questions about the reading passage.

1. Who launched the first artificial satellite?
   (a) NASA was the first one to do so
   (b) The Soviet Union launched the first artificial satellite called Sputnik
   (c) Japan

2. When did the Space Age dawn?
   (a) It dawned only after 1986
   (b) The Space Age dawned in 1957
   (c) In 1962

3. Which are the lead countries in Space business?
   (a) Super Powers like USA, Japan
   (b) Asian countries like China, India
   (c) Both (a) (b)

4. Why should revenues from Space business rise in trillions?
   (a) Because interplanetary enterprise is enjoying a rise in popularity
   (b) Because the Pentagon became its new customer
   (c) Because of the surgein private startups offering low-cost, effective solutions

5. What does the concluding sentence tell us?
   (a) Soon our children or grandchildren will educate us
   (b) School children will soon have space excursions
   (c) If empowered well, Space Business will develop at a meteoric scale

Writing about the Article

Answer each question based on the reading passage.

1. Which space exploration problems are listed in the lesson?

2. How has each one of the following contributed in Space field?
   India –

   Japan -

3. What should we do to advance borderless commercial space business?

The Space Business

Across

3 At present, we are unable to move past _____ rivalries.
8 This estimation is rooted in the _____ in private startups.
9 The _____ enterprise is enjoying a rise in popularity.
10 In 1962, private _____ ventured into the cosmos.

Down

1 Private entities ventured into the _____ to fully contribute to the promising economy.
2 To advance commercial pursuits, we need to increase the _____ study of the cosmos.
4 The space business has global _____ nearing $385 billion.
5 The space business is a _____ field.
6 The human collective was not able to make good on their _____.
7 Space _____ has problems such as cosmic debris.

WORD LIST

AMBITION   ENTITIES   INTERPLANETARY   SURGE   COLLABORATIVE
EXPLORATION   LUCRATIVE   COSMOS   GEOPOLITICAL   REVENUES

98

Pre-Reading questions | **Discuss these questions in pairs.**

1. What do you know about the power of a Passport?
2. How do you define a strong passport?
3. What would help increase Japan's number of overseas students?

What are your thoughts? | 考えましょう

1. Strength is equal to having an important document and being able to use it.
    Agree Disgree

2. An individual's position abroad depends upon the position of the sending country.
   Agree Disgree

3. A passport is an economic asset.

   Agree Disgree

Passport Strength

Passport strength refers to the ability of the passport holder to travel and enter various countries without restrictions. The importance of a passport cannot be overstated. With globalization and technological advancements, there have been some significant changes.

Strong passports such as those from Canada *(184) and the United States (185) allow their citizens to travel visa-free around the world. According to the global citizenship and residence advisory firm Henley & Partners (2021), some of the most powerful passports are those of Japan, Singapore (192), Germany, and South Korea (190), among others. Meanwhile, weaker passports, such as those of Afghanistan (26), make traveling abroad much more difficult because travelers face a visa barrier. In this context, nations often grant visa exemptions because reducing paperwork can bring in steady flows of deep-pocketed foreigners. Streams of people bring economic benefits in various forms and improve the status of a country with its peers. The receiving country considers several critical factors before granting visa exemptions for specific nations, such as the economic position of the sending country, diplomatic ties, and refugee flows.

Regardless of a person's passport, the most important thing is whether it can be used to access education. A powerful passport will be easier to use to enter higher education or find employment abroad. In the case of Japan, the country with "the world's most powerful passport," only 24% of citizens are passport holders, the lowest proportion among rich countries. Most people feel uncomfortable with the idea of experiencing a new world. Several factors prevent them from traveling, including limited annual leave, food restrictions, hygiene concerns, and safety. Most importantly, there is fear of discomfort from not being understood. In recent days, even retired pensioners, who have abundant free time and money, travel less than their parents. Until the 1990s, Japanese people were excited to wander the world. Youths took a month- or week-long tour with copies of *Chikyu No Arukikata* (How to Walk the Earth), a favorite travel guide. All because a strong yen made their journey practical and possible.

The increasing cost of studying abroad (approximately $30,000 annually) no longer represents an inexpensive deal for Japanese families. Indeed, wealthy, highly educated parents know the benefits of using a passport to study abroad for financial stability. The ability to study and gain work experience abroad is entirely dependent on what passport one has, i.e., one's citizenship. According to Forbes magazine 2017, 42% of citizens in the US and 76% of people in England held a passport. It shows how citizens' lifestyles change with exploration or their willingness to experience the world.

In general, many politicians and people in business prefer that their children study abroad. Building human capital from an early age provides lifetime assets. Business deals and political ties are based on trust, and the period people know each other. After all, holding something powerful and making the best use of it is a real strength.

* The numbers (26) to (192) indicate the number of countries in which citizens enjoy visa exemption.

Tomorrow belongs to people who prepare for it today.
<u>African Proverb</u>

Vocabulary List. （辞書必要、必ず辞書を参照してください）

No.	Word	Definition	Definition in my language	Synonyms
1	strength (n.)			asset, capability
2	overstated (adj.)			excessive, flashy
3	influential (adj.)			effective, powerful
4	steady (adj.)			frequently, regularity
5	deep pockets (n.)			assets, prosperity
6	alliance (n.)			diplomatic ties, peers, treaty
7	predominantly (adv.)			mainly, most importantly
8	substantial (adj.)			massive, powerful, vast
9	hygiene (n.)			clean, pure, sanitary
10	wander (v.)			cruise, shift

Definition

a. very widespread or common
b. abundance of financial resources
c. absolutely or immaculately clean or pure
d. a formal agreement between two or more nations or organizations
e. presented too grandly or prominently
f. occurring regularly or usually
g. to walk or move in a leisurely or aimless way
h. a good or beneficial quality or attribute of a person or thing
i. important or powerful in rank, position or status
j. significant in amount, level or degree

Vocabulary Review

Fill in the blanks with the words from the box below. Change the form of the words if necessary.

1. strength	2. overstated	3. influential	4. overseas
5. restriction	6. alliance	7. predominantly	8. substantial
9. hygiene	10. wander		

1. They have high standards of food _____.

2. Mark _____ like a cloud from one place to another.

3. A _____ amount of cash was robbed from the house.

4. Vitamin C comes _____ from raw fruit.

5. She is an _____ person in the society.

6. Many _____ start with huge goals.

7. Covid-19 has brought many _____ on normal life.

8. Unity is a nation's _____.

9. Many of her assignments come from _____.

10. He _____ the usefulness of his product.

Idioms about *Passport Strength*

Idioms	Meaning
deep pockets	abundance of financial resources
passport to	that which allows one access to something desirable
to come into play	to become an important factor

Please choose the correct idioms from above.

1. ABC, the NGO is known to have _____.

2. How well you can foresee will _____ when deciding on a career.

3. Knowing a foreign language can be your _____ successful settling in that land.

Check your Understanding
Answer the following questions about the reading passage.

1. What is the central idea?
   (a) Until the 1990s, Japanese people were excited to wander the world; now they don't
   (b) Holding a strong passport and making the best use of it is real strength
   (c) Japanese travelers can visit 192 countries and territories without a visa

2. Who send/s their children abroad despite increasing education costs there?
   (a) Government employees
   (b) Teachers
   (c) Many politicians and business people

3. Which factors prevent people from experiencing a new world?
   (a) Limited annual leave, safety concerns, ethnic cuisines and hygiene
   (b) An annoying fear of the discomfort of not being understood
   (c) Both (a) & (c)

4. Why do nations often grant visa exemptions?
   (a) Because there are streams of people flowing-in
   (b) Because it can bring in steady flows of deep-pocketed foreigners
   (c) So that travelers face barriers

5. Who allow/s their citizens to travel visa-free around the world?
   (a) Afghanistan
   (b) Henley & Partners
   (c) Canada and the United States

Writing about the Article
Answer each question based on the reading passage.

1. In this lesson, "passport" is synonymous with _____.

2. How did the travelling trends of each of the following change?
   Youth of 1990s-

   Retired Pensioners –

3. Why do many politicians and businesspeople want their children to study abroad?

Interesting facts (Passport Strength)

1. Passports have been started to use officially since 13th century.
2. USA citizens can apply for passports in post office or even in public libraries.
3. After facial recognition technology implementation, smiling photo is banned on the passport.

Note

Pre-Reading questions | Discuss these questions in pairs.

1. What do you know about Fake News?
2. Which source of news do you prefer?
3. What solutions do you have for controlling false news?

What are your thoughts?	考えましょう

1. Quality news is relayed for educating people.

   Agree   Disagree

2. Mere popular news should be limited.

   Agree   Disagree

3. If you cultivate independent thinking, you can make better decisions.

   Agree   Disagree

Fake News

Fake news is a universally present and notorious concept in the internet age. Today, political parties, news outlets, and propaganda groups have no morals about spreading misinformation. Anyone on the internet can broadcast made-up "facts" with no verified sources or quotations.

5   Contrary to popular belief, the concept of fake news is not novel. The word "misinformation" has been around since the late 16th century. The spread of those types of news was rampant in the early modern period and was an essential issue for the leading philosophers of the era. For example, Francis Bacon discussed the dangers of confirmation bias in his Novum Organum (1620).

10   Today, the body of false news is denser than that of actual news stories. Those who spread these false stories often base them on personal beliefs, making it more challenging to separate fact from fiction. Fake news often uses deliberately sensitive and aggressive language to hide the fact that it is falsified.

First, such news exists within a complex ecosystem of disinformation and misinformation. These stories are often twisted and broadcast by political parties and policymakers to 15   sway public opinion. Misinformation is inaccurate statistics or facts mistakenly spread by undisciplined journalists without the intent to cheat. With the help of technological convenience, such content can easily be spread by sharing it on social media, blogs, and sites such as Wikipedia.

Second, bots and websites that publish clickbait content also spread half-truths. Economically 20   driven gossip sites and platforms use false statements to generate clicks. The internet has also revived long-refuted conspiracies, such as the flat earth theory. The internet makes it easy to find fanatics and deceive them as they form online communities.

In conclusion, relying on verified sources in such confusing times is critical. One must use reputable publications to fact-check data, as this is the only way to reduce the wide 25   broadcasting of fake news. Ultimately, everyone is free to judge, analyze and think independently. The final judgment or decision varies from person to person depending on the individual's analytical skills, ethnicity, family background, and wisdom.

Seeing is different from being told.

African proverb

Vocabulary List.　（辞書必要、必ず辞書を参照してください）

No.	Word	Definition	Definition in my language	Synonyms
1	notorious (adj.)			disreputable, infamous
2	propaganda (n.)			misinformation, publicity, promotion
3	rampant (adj.)			unbridled, uncontrolled
4	dense (adj.)			significantly larger, thick
5	sensitive (adj.)			inflammatory
6	sway (v.)			affect, influence, swing
7	clickbait (n.)			enticement, lure, temptation (to get clicks), trap
8	rebirth (n.)			regeneration, revived
9	conspiracy (n.)			connivance, plot, scheme
10	cheating (n.)			con, deceiving

Definition

a. period of new growth, activity

b. content whose main purpose is to attract attention and encourage visitors to click on a link to a particular web page

c. widely known for something typically bad quality or deed

d. a secret plan by a group to do something unlawful or harmful

e. rhythmic movement side to side, to influence

f. quick to respond to slight changes or influences

g. something closely packed together

h. information of a biased or misleading nature, used to promote a political cause

i. spreading unchecked (especially of something unwelcome)

j. act dishonestly or unfairly in order to gain something

Vocabulary Review

Fill in the blanks with the words from the box below. Change the form of the words if necessary.

1. notorious	2. propaganda	3. rampant	4. dense
5. sensitive	6. sway	7. clickbait	8. rebirth
9. conspiracy	10. cheating		

1. Corruption is _____ in his office.

2. Their _____ told people that everything in the West was bad.

3. Some people believe in _____.

4. The company is _____ for paying its bills late.

5. Copying in exams is _____ .

6. The trees _____ slightly in the wind.

7. Mimosa is a plant _____ to touch.

8. Due to adequate rainfall there are _____ forests in this zone.

9. The CIA uncovered _____ against the government.

10. The expert asked startups to skip _____ lists and create something genuine.

Idioms about *Fake News*

Idioms	Meaning
fake off	to waste time
cheat sheet	a piece of paper with information so as to be used in exams
pearls of wisdom	something that is very wise and helpful

Please choose the correct idioms from above.

1. She was caught using a(n) _____ during the final test, hence she failed.

2. Ron's grandmother shared with her _____ so Ron has changed.

3. Hey guys! Stop _____ and get to work!!

Interesting facts (Fake News)

1. Study shows a news website can spread fake news faster than real news.

2. In general, it is hard to tell the difference between real and fake news.

3. Trusting false information could lead to damaging your physical or mental health.

Check your Understanding
Answer the following questions about the reading passage.

1. What is the main idea?
   (a) News often uses sensitive and salty language to hide the facts
   (b) It is critical to rely on verified sources in order to curb Fake news
   (c) The concept of hoax news is not novel

2. When was Novum Organum written by Francis Bacon?
   (a) During recent times
   (b) After the 17th century
   (c) In 1620

3. Where does twisted news exist?
   (a) It exists within a complex ecosystem of disinformation and misinformation
   (b) Only in political publications
   (c) Light magazines

4. Why is click bait content used?
   (a) Click bait content is used to revive truth
   (b) Bots, websites and gossip sites that publish "click bait" content are used to spread half-truth
   (c) Click bait content is used to reduce misinformation

5. Who often twists news stories?
   (a) Social media, blogs, websites etc
   (b) News channels
   (c) Political parties, policy makers and propaganda groups

Writing about the Article
Answer each question based on the reading passage.

1. In this lesson, what is meant by final judgment?

2. How to define the following words/terms?
   misinformation –

   click bait content –

   long-refuted –

3. Why is it critical to rely on verified sources?

Fake News

Across

3 Today, political parties, news outlets have no _____ about spreading misinformation.

4 Fact-checking data alone can cut through the _____ distribution of fake news.

5 The spread of hoax news was _____ in the Renaissance.

6 Distorted news often uses _____ language to hide its falsification.

7 Misinformation is spread of inaccurate facts mistakenly without the intent of _____.

9 In the _____ spread of hoax news was a severe issue for leading philosophers.

Down

1 Today, _____ groups have no scruples about spreading misinformation.

2 The internet has also revived long-refuted _____.

8 News is often twisted to _____ public opinion.

10 Bots and websites that write "_____" content spread misinformation.

WORD LIST

CLICKBAIT	DENSE	RAMPANT	SWAY	CONSPIRACIES
INFLAMMATORY	RENAISSANCE	DECEPTION	PROPAGANDA	SCRUPLES

The "American Dream" was, is and will continue to be the driving force of economic success in the United States. Arguably, this is the first nation founded on the (　　　　) idea that "all men are created equal." In 1776, the Founding Fathers promised life, liberty, and the pursuit of happiness to many immigrants.

The meaning of the American Dream has changed over time. By the 1930s, it meant a successful career, home ownership, upward (　　　　), and wealth. Essentially, it represented equal opportunity regardless of family history or social (　　　). For those willing to work hard, a good life was attainable.

The Lehman shock of 2008 impacted the meaning of the American Dream. It became less about (　　　　) wealth and more about living a meaningful life. Time spent with friends and family creating warm memories became the (　　　　) of a fulfilling life.

In the 21st century, many believe (　　　　) and success are no longer easily achievable. Expensive housing and rising healthcare and higher education costs make upward mobility and wealth challenging to achieve. Others believe that the American Dream remains alive. Baby Boomers define this dream as having a large house and the financial means to raise a family. Generation X sees it as achieving professional success based on knowledge, wisdom and a well-paying job with (　　　). Millennials view the American Dream as enjoying their lives by pursuing a passion and focusing less on (　　　　).

Many countries, such as Japan, have the opportunity to create their own version of the American Dream by thinking outside the box. Indeed, the immigration of highly skilled labor is a promising solution to Japan's shrinking workforce due to the country's aging population. Japan's low crime rates, high quality of life, and rich culture make it an attractive place to live and raise a family. Therefore, the aspiration of living a happy life can be (　　　　) in any part of the world that welcomes (　　　　) searching for a better life.

(monumental, mobility, status, accumulating, cornerstones, prosperity, benefits, consumerism, reproduced, immigrants)

Listening Exercise

The (   ) of educated professionals from one country to another in search of a better standard of living and access to advanced technology is known as brain drain. In the past, low-skilled laborers from around the globe (   ) (   ). Gradually, the labor needs of the receiving nations shifted toward workers with advanced skills. Since that time, many immigrants have made similar journeys.

As industrialization advanced, demand for white-collar workers was partially met by specialists from other countries. In the mid-1940s, Western Europe saw its scientific elite and other experts relocating to the United States. They were attracted by higher salaries and more advanced facilities. Since 1970, the need for information technology (IT) specialists has (   ) tenfold as Silicon Valley became the global hub. In the last decade, the demand for healthcare workers has increased by approximately 60% worldwide. Currently, healthcare workers and IT specialists from Asia are the most prominent subjects of brain drain. This remains (   ) as demand for human (   ) continues in developed countries.

While developed countries fill the gap with immigrants, home countries experience consequences. They invest considerable time and money in education, and the departure of those holding advanced degrees often causes a shortage of skilled labor. In addition, the (   ) of tax revenue slows economic growth and increases inequities between nations. As a result, funds for research and development are insufficient; hence countries cannot achieve comparable technological and scientific achievements. Nevertheless, there are also positive effects of brain drain. For example, financial (   ) contribute significantly to the GDP of home countries.

As per the International Organization for Migration (IOM), $121 billion was received in remittances in 2000 and $714 billion in 2019. Which is 20 times higher than the amount in 1980 ($37 billion). Additionally, due to global communication, foreign-born workers are no longer (   ) from their home towns. Consequently, innovations multiply as migrants create professional networks with entrepreneurs in their country of origin. This circular flow of information is defined as brain circulation.

Brain drain will continue to be a reality, but not without a human cost. Professionals making the journey abroad leave behind their country, culture, customs, family, and friends. Nonetheless, one person's hopes and dreams for a better standard of living are another person's inspiration. Those left behind aspire to achieve higher levels of education to make their dreams a reality.

(exodus, supported, industrialization, increased, persistent, capital, loss, inequities, remittances, isolated)

Medical treatment typically used to be a local affair. Now, it is a (   ) globalized business. Since 4,000 B.C.E., aesthetic journeys have been made to (   ), (   ) hot springs known for their health benefits. In ancient times, health spas sprang up in Switzerland, Greece, India and Rome. Maintaining a healthy lifestyle and youthful appearance remain just as important today as they were 6,000 years ago.

The healing waters of the past were the predecessors of future cosmetic tourism. Cosmetic tourism combines medical procedures with a vacation in an attractive destination such as Mexico or Thailand. Why do people spend so much time and money trying to look their best? Research indicates that being attractive has its perks. Attractive people are more likely to be hired for a job. Good looks are also associated with positive characteristics such as trustworthiness, intelligence, prosperity, and authority.

Economic (   ) thus make people flock to foreign countries for cosmetic procedures. Breast (   ), rhinoplasty, and eyelid surgery can cost 50%-70% less than in their home countries. According to the International Society of (   ) Plastic Surgery, over 27 million people traveled abroad for cosmetic operations in 2016—86.2% of whom were women. The Organization for Economic Cooperation and Development (OECD 2021) forecasted an annual increase of 25% in the next ten years.

While medical procedures can be far less expensive abroad, there are some downsides. Most insurance companies will not cover cross-border operations, forcing travelers to pay out-of-pocket. (   ) care can be poor and can lead to (   ) and even death. In some cases, patients experience medical malpractice that leaves them permanently disfigured or needing corrective surgery.

Despite these pitfalls, foreign markets are benefiting in cosmetic tourism. New cosmetic surgery centers are (   ) worldwide, and insurance carriers are offering cross-border health plans. India offers a medical visa (MED Visa) for medical procedures with travel insurance. Bookimed is a medical tourism agency that pairs patients with all-inclusive packages for medical care overseas. Such developments should make foreign medical treatments more appealing. After all, cultural knowledge and language skills are needed to secure international customer satisfaction. These factors are often neglected by cosmetic tourism (   ). When the fulfillment of these requirements can be promised and delivered, it will enhance the business of a nation.

(systematically, therapeutic, mineral-rich, incentives, augmentation, Aesthetic, Post-operative, infections, popping up, providers)

In general, everyone wants to start their day "right," usually with something familiar, whatever that may be. According to one English traveler to the USA in the 1820s, most 19th-century citizens enjoyed astonishingly heavy breakfasts. In addition to tea, coffee, cold ham, and beef, "hot fish, sausages, beefsteaks, broiled fowls, fried and stewed oysters, and preserved fruits" were also common. Such a (   ) start to the day may have been suitable in the past when most people spent their days plowing fields. Such rich food before running to a desk job can lead to "the great American stomachache."

Over the last century, human eating habits have changed dramatically and for the better. The ways we shop, cook, and eat have been (   ) and (   ) to align with our new knowledge and life goals. After the Industrial Revolution, people moved from farms to factories and offices, where much time was spent sitting or standing in one place. The heavy breakfasts that were useful before work on the farm and would now cause upset stomachs fell out of favor.

Today, eating on the go is on the rise. Some critics say that for most of human history, grocery stores did not exist. Modern eating patterns come from advertising and multinational corporations (MNCs), insisting that people eat bacon or cereal first, every morning. Various academic research findings suggest skipping this early meal affects (   ) disorders in young women. Skipping breakfast can (   ) academic performance or cause psychological distress in young students, affecting their (   ) achievement. On the contrary, healthy eating habits help to maintain a body mass index (BMI) within the normal range.

Business leaders often prefer morning breakfast meetings for effective (   ) and decision-making. After all, alcohol leads to an altered mindset; most of the time, if alcohol is involved, actual business does not get done. Have you ever thought about how breakfast differs in other countries? While grains, (   ), and fruit are common in many parts of the world, they are served differently according to climate and altitude. In the Indian state of Maharashtra, a typical morning meal is *kande pohe*, made with pre-soaked dry rice flakes. The flakes, roasted with chilies, onions, mustard seeds, cumin and curry leaves, (   ) liquids quickly and are easily digested. In Vietnam, the most (   ) and popular food is *pho* rice noodles and beef soup with aromatic herbs, lime, crunchy sprouts and spicy chilies, all cooked together in the comforting heat of the soup.

In short, an energy-fueled start makes a difference in decision-making in day-to-day life. Even when one does not have time, one can eat something small on the way to work, for instance, fruit, sandwiches, or homemade rice balls for a decent start.

(substantial, optimized, monitored, menstrual, impact, cognitive, persuasion, breads, absorb, iconic)

Whenever humans interact romantically, the modern media want to nose in. Until recently, romantic matches were established through parents, priests, friends, or professional ( ). These intermediaries would match couples based on their characteristics or personal ( ). The attraction of the partners was based on their social status or physical attractiveness. From there, a bond was created, which could later grow into a healthy romance or even ( ) marriage.

Today, however, internet technology has given rise to new ways to interact. With such developments, paternal institutions are being broken down as well. As modernity and gender equality have advanced, people have begun to take ownership of their own lives. Now, the multiple options available for finding a partner present a certain magic charm. One can find happiness in any part of the world. Dating apps have taken the global stage by ( ): the dating app industry has been valued at over 7 billion dollars per year. These apps match people with compatible personality characteristics. Dr. Dyrenforth asked 20,000 people about their relationships and personalities. Couples with similar mindsets were indeed happier and more successful than those with dissimilar mindsets. Are dating apps then the future of love or just money-making mechanisms?

Our environment has made physical interaction a luxury since the modern work ethic has turned people into workaholics. With this, ( ) interactions have been reduced. Further, match-making sites got a ( ). People with poor social skills tend to experience more stress and loneliness and prefer to use these services. Finding a perfect match is always challenging on dating sites. Sudden disappearances, silence, ghosting and failure to respond to texts or emails are widespread. Overdependence on these sites may result in disappointment.

The basics of finding a partner have not changed with time or digital tools. First, the best way to meet the perfect partner is to be excited and be oneself. Do things that one is passionate about and are ( ) and personally ( ). This puts you in a position to meet a significant other with similar interests, opening the door to conversation. Second, let friends know that you are available. Accept all invitations to parties, engage in group activities that you like most, or go hiking, biking, or horse riding.

Finally, nothing pulls us down like the feeling of being rejected. Indeed, we must look at rejection as a ( ) to successful relationships. Nevertheless, when rejection happens, anyone feels ( ) about it. This forceful energy can work as a fuel for you to become so successful that the one who has denied your love will regret the loss.

(matchmakers, assumption, true, storm, substantial, boom, appealing, enriching, stepping stone, spiteful)

People do not choose to be disabled. An estimated one billion people, approximately 15% of the world's population, live with a special need of some kind. Not all disorders are visible. In some parts of the world, people with disabilities have equal access to education, healthcare, and employment and are, therefore, able to be productive members of society. This was not always the case.

For a long time, people in Ghana regarded a child with a disability as a bad (   ). Such kid was believed to be caused by parents' (   ), (   ), or (   ). Families visited medicine men for healing. A (   ) would be given for the disabled person to drink, almost always resulting in death. In Kyrgyzstan, families that did not have money to care for their unfit children had to institutionalize them. Sadly, these children were neglected and uneducated due to a lack of funding. They were tied to beds or locked in cages. They were viewed as (   ), less than humans. In extreme cases, medical experimentation was performed on them without their or their family's (   ).

In 2006, the United Nations Convention on the Rights of Persons with Disabilities (CRPD) was created to improve the quality of life of people with special needs. Since that time, 181 nations have (   ) the CRPD. In Ghana, the killing of such children was abolished. In Kyrgyzstan, these students are now attending public schools. Like many other CRPD countries, Kyrgyzstan is removing barriers to education and employment by building (   ) and elevators. Additionally, organizations are being formed to help support disabled people in finding and sustaining employment.

The future looks brighter for these people as the value they bring to society is becoming more visible. Employers in the United States have seen an increase in production and sales by matching jobs to people with the right skills and abilities. Japan recently established its first talent agency for people with special needs, Co-Co Life Talent Division. The Paralympics, which highlight serious athletes, are now held alongside the Olympic Games. Australia's Madeline Stuart walks runways worldwide as the first professional model with Down syndrome. The contributions of people with special needs are beginning to be (   ) globally, but we still have a long way to go.

(omen, sins, evildoing, witchcraft, potion, inferior, consent, ratified, ramps, embraced)

Listening Exercise

Food diplomacy is a tool that uses food and cuisine to mend political divides, (   ) relationships, and break down barriers. This activity can (   ) everyone from heads of state to the family unit. Food is more than just (   ); it represents a person's national identity, culture, and heritage.

Culinary diplomacy has been used since ancient times and continues to be used today. Ancient Greece solidified negotiations and peace treaties over wine and lunch with foreign leaders. In ancient Rome, peace was made with enemies through a shared meal. Former US president Ronald Reagan (1981-1989) served former leader of the Soviet Union, Mikhail Gorbachev (1985-1991), Russian caviar and wine from the Russian River Valley in California to offer a sign of respect and honor the influence of Russian immigrants in this area. The soft power of food has been (   ) for millennia.

In the early 21st century (2002-2003), food began to be used to positively influence international perspectives through nation branding. The aim was increasing countries' cultural influence through food. Thailand, for example, began promoting its unique cuisine worldwide in hopes of increasing exports, tourism, and international (   ) of Thai food and culture. Since the campaign began, the number of Thai restaurants has increased from 5,500 (2001) to 15,000 (2019), and tourism has increased by 200%. Other countries have used similar nation-branding strategies, such as Japan, Malaysia, Peru, South Korea, Taiwan, and even North Korea.

While food can be used to (   ) social ties and reduce (   ), not every conflict can be solved in this way. Disputes of some nations are so significant that leaders are not yet ready to negotiate a solution around the dinner table. In other cases, leaders are simply not interested in (   ) food. In these scenarios, this type of diplomacy cannot work.

Overall, the use of food diplomacy is exploding across the globe as a serious tool for international relations in both the public and private sectors. Universities are beginning to develop courses around the power of food, such as "Conflict Cuisine: An Introduction to War and Peace Around the Dinner Table" by Johanna Mendelson-Forman of the American University's School of International Service. Des Moines Public School (   ) out the traditional parent-teacher conferences for Culture Night, when teachers and student's families bond over a shared meal from the students' home countries.

Whether connecting governments or citizens, the soft power of food continues to be a successful tool for breaking down barriers. It has the power to foster (   ) and make friends of enemies. It goes without saying that culinary diplomacy will continue to grow as a valuable tool in international relations.

(foster, involve, sustenance, leveraged, recognition, strengthen, hostility, delicious, tossed, compassion)

Frequently, immigrants reached new (   ) with only the clothes on their backs and hope welling in their hearts. This story of migration continues to repeat with new causes, be they economic, social, political, or environmental. During pre-World War II, elites such as scientists, philosophers, leaders and political figures migrated to save their own lives. Since then, there have been waves of mass migratory movements.

Subsequently, these non-natives work hard, struggle to settle, and (   ) in a new land as guests. While bringing up their own children, they transfer to them the value of this struggle. From their homelands, migrants bring knowledge, unique work styles and innovative ideas based on patience and compromises.

This effort is reflected in 2nd-generation migrants (   ) these values and growing into solid personalities. (   ) these values, they grow into successful adults. According to the Pew Research Center, second-generation Hispanic and Asian immigrants in the USA do better than their parents in terms of household income ($58,000 versus $46,000), the acquisition of higher education (36% versus 29%), and homeownership (64% versus 51%). 2nd-generation Indian and Chinese immigrants in London have done very well educationally. They have (   ) themselves from restaurant service or factory work jobs. High-earning professionals such as entrepreneurs, doctors, professors and even Parliament members are typical examples of outsiders. For decades, members of the second generation have had a major impact on their nation's destiny.

In regard to 3rd-generation immigrants, there are typically fewer advancements. In general, they cannot be more or even as successful as previous generations. Since they already start from a more prosperous position. After all, struggling can never be the same as reading or hearing about it. The 3rd generation sees a natural gap between their lifestyles.

When an immigrant generation works hard, the fruits of its labor can be reaped and enjoyed by the next two generations. If these (   ) want to prosper further, they must build upon their own legacy. They need to (   ) and nurture the gains. There is a need to predict and navigate the next 100 years.

The liberal and humanitarian world accepts immigrants and promises them (   ). Now, it is up to migrants to (   ) this offer to (   ) through hard work, focus and discipline. In conclusion, building an empire was not easy for our ancestors; maintaining and protecting it is a constant challenge for the next generations.

(shores, flourish, developing, Imbibing, liberated, descendants, toil, prosperity, leverage, achieve success)

Choosing to live alone and unmarried is a way of life. Asian culture attaches (   ) weight to the idea that families should live under one roof. Being single is still considered (   ) and taboo in many societies and cultures. Inarguably, the share of people who remain single has been (   ) in newly industrialized countries. Being single is a brave choice in a world where adulthood is often considered equal to marriage and children.

In 17th-century New England, the state placed social and economic sanctions on unmarried individuals. As a result, even respected single women who devoted their lives to serving society were labeled (   ), a rather hurtful term. Moreover, traditionally, unmarried men have had more freedom than unmarried women. Unattached men have been labeled bachelors and have not been rejected by society. Meanwhile, unmarried women have been labeled old maids. Society has tried to (   ) them to the care giving roles of wife and mother rather than seeing them as individuals. Even in the 19th century, American society had not accepted men and women who chose to remain unattached. As of 2020, very few Hindus and Muslims live alone.

(   ) in the 21st century, singledom can be recognized in socially and culturally diverse countries such as the United States, and the European countries. "Single culture," labeled the *Ohitorisama* Movement, has risen in Japan. Although not everyone is affected by this shift, the community has started viewing singlehood as a diverse lifestyle. Today, educated, unattached women have more freedom and opportunities to pursue their dreams. As a result, they have better career (   ) than before.

Despite its continued (   ), staying single has many benefits. They are being able to explore one's individuality and personal development. This can offer time and freedom for (   ) relationships. It allows one to travel alone on a (   ) and explore the world. Without a romantic relationship, a person can focus on health and financial well-being. On the other hand, loneliness may cast doubt on life choices. With age, single adults face increasing societal pressure to settle down. They may also struggle with a lack of intimacy and romantic attachment.

Ultimately, our society needs to accept singledom as a positive lifestyle choice. We must allow our youth to relish their singledom so that they can grow as complete individuals. Only this can lead to a developed society and then a nation.

(enormous, odd, escalating, spinsters, restrict, Today, aspirations, stigmatization, platonic, whim)

Humans are creatures that seek knowledge and information, very similarly to the way animals receive rewards from food for survival. (Indeed, the genetic difference between chimpanzees and humans is just 2%.) Humans know how to store and use this knowledge to improve the future. Smartphones are one of the best examples of this capability. Steve Jobs announced the iPhone in 2007, launching our lives 50 years ahead in the technology world.

The iPhone did not come out until six months after its initial (   ). During this time Apple turned Jobs's prototype into a mass-marketable gadget. When it finally hit stores in June, people lined up outside stores to buy one, and 270,000 phones were sold in the first two days. From there, the story of the iPhone has been one of (   ), not (   ).

Millions of people use an iPhone as their only computer, camera, GPS device, music player, means of communication, and payment tool. It puts the world in our pockets. This offers us benefits, but it certainly challenges us in many (   ) ways as well. There is (   ) debate on how smartphones (   ) the association between modern technology and our biology. This universally accepted, (   ) device has fundamentally changed us. It has been seen as (   ) to concentration, sleep patterns and eyesight.

On the other hand, with the help of smartphones, scientists are trying new ways to improve the attention of children suffering from ADHD. In addition, various apps have been developed that can, for example, (   ) one's sleep or check one's stress (   ), which might improve how students' brains work in the classroom. With careful consideration, we can imagine how technology can amplify opportunities to care for other human beings.

After all, whether to be the slave or the master of the smartphone is up to the individual. Therefore, what can be done to keep smartphones in their place? One can start with digital dieting, which is similar to avoiding junk food and irregular eating habits. The idea is to control the abundance of junk information and choose to have more disciplined browsing habits. One could avoid texting, say, on weekends or Friday and show one's phone who is the boss.

(reveal, evolution, revolution, fundamental, endless, amplify, everyday, harmful, track, level)

(   ) is the fundamental human strength of "paying attention, on purpose, in the present moment, without judging." It helps us realize and (   ) the best part of ourselves as human beings. It is a practice involved in various religious and secular traditions from Hinduism and Buddhism and, more recently, nonreligious meditations. Some argue that the history of mindfulness is also rooted in Judaism, Christianity and Islam.

In the 1970s, Jon Kabat-Zinn founded the Center for Mindfulness at the University of Massachusetts Medical School. He made it known to the world. Some people are always physically or mentally busy. In addition, technology leads us to want to be connected and have something to do, leaving few occasions to just "be."

(   ) has become fundamental to our generation. We often text while watching TV and look at our phone while walking on the sidewalk. Likewise, even after office hours, people often bring work home. The more we do, the more stressed we feel. For example, modern educators and students (   ). Fulfilling academic and social expectations is demanding. Although our world is moving and changing faster than ever, students are facing new challenges. This affects their ability to focus, regulate emotions, build inner (   ) and form healthy and supportive relationships. In developed countries, nearly 1 in 3 students experience (   ) by the age of 18. Nearly 40% of high school students feel lonely and left out. In the USA, 46% of all children have experienced (   ). There is a solution to every problem. We usually need only time, money, or personal attention to resolve it. No problem falls outside the reach of these factors. So, (   ) to find the right solution.

Mindfulness comes in many different forms, such as yoga, Zen practice or even washing dishes. As Thich Nhat Hanh (   ) paying attention to the purpose is the essential part. According to Duke University of Medical Research data, among US practitioners, an hour of yoga per week reduces stress levels. This ultimately cuts an individual's healthcare costs by an average of $2,000 yearly.

In a world of constant stress and disruption, simply sitting still and relaxing for a while is essential. It has (   ) become part of the self-help movement. One should start each day with a must-do list, step away from screen at specific times and focus on one thing at a time. Stress can strike at any time, so practising meditation daily is the ultimate solution.

(Mindfulness, enhance, Multitasking, carry so much on their shoulders, resilience, anxiety, trauma, stay grounded, advocates, gradually)

🎧 13

Society comes before individuals, so humans must satisfy specific basic needs to survive. As he became a (   ) social being, coupling and living together as a community became even more vital. Therefore, the arrangement of marriage is an (   ) of trust between two individuals. Today, individuals marry for emotional, (   ), financial, and religious purposes. This knot, which some believe is tied in heaven, often (   ), and its (   ) is continually threatened. Nevertheless, the bond of marriage has (   ) the benefit of partnership and ideal stability.

Historically, for economic reasons, a gendered division of labor was implemented. Consequently, men started earning money and obtaining property. So, women became responsible for the domestic tasks of childcare and raising families. With the rise of patriarchy, womenfolk suffered denial. Their labor and skills were undervalued and seen as weak and dependent. With modernization, however, this gender bias is healing. (   ), educated womenfolk became far more powerful. Their monetary (   ) insured them from being exploited by their male counterparts. Thus, (   ) gives them more equality and perhaps more satisfaction.

This holds true only for those male partners who can appreciate and welcome this change. It is a conflict and a loss of the "perfect" union for those who do not. With financial independence, women now have enough space to run if marriage causes them trouble. They do not want to compromise to sustain a troublesome marriage.

Today, separation rates are increasing (65%- 70% of couples in America); hence people are eager to help those undergoing such separation. Governments, too, may be supportive since they know from research that broken families stress the entire system, leading to a physically and mentally sick public. This view is even more widespread in Asia. In an interview in 1994, Lee Kuan Yew, former prime minister of Singapore, said that stable marriages make a sustainable and sound society. It means a happy family, creating a stable next generation. This stable generation is the foundation of a strong nation. He feared that collapse of the family would be the main threat to the success of Singapore.

To save the collapse, the responsibility is on both partners. They may draw support from their elders (parents and in-laws) or externally from professional counselors. There are many ways to strengthen a marriage, but the will to do so is the most basic requirement.

One could look at this issue differently: How about loving, marrying, and committing to oneself before another person? It means to love ourselves the way we want our partners to love us. After all, love blossoms through patience and tolerance, for a genuinely (   ) relationship of giving and taking.

(rational, enhancement, libidinal, frays, permanence, embodied, Ironically, empowerment, wedlock, profound)

In an increasingly connected world, proficiency in a foreign language is an unquestionable asset. Even though learning an unfamiliar (   ) can be challenging, it opens up a world of possibilities and presents numerous academic, professional, and social benefits. Before World War I, regional (   ) was a cherished skill. People worldwide are (   ) about various local (   ); however, there was a massive shift in our perception of languages during and after WW II. English (   ) gained political and cultural predominance in many post-colonial countries, making people lose the will to learn new vocabulary.

Nevertheless, interest in learning new languages grew from 1950 to 1990. Today, multilingualism is once again considered an undeniable advantage. The current political and social encouragement is toward diversity. This has inspired many individuals to engage with new lexicons of which they are not native speakers.

There are many benefits to learning a new language in today's highly interconnected global landscape. Mastering a second language is a gateway to exploring new cultures and international communities. It is considered a valuable skill in job applications to pursue overseas academic and work opportunities. Employers prefer to hire international applicants who are (   ) in the employer's tongue. It also helps one explore untranslated literature from different global communities that would otherwise be inaccessible. It also allows people to expand their worldview and connect with unique individuals from other communities.

Moreover, there are many (   ) benefits attached. These include developing critical thinking, boosting memory, enhanced problem solving, and increased creativity and multitasking ability. Picking up a second language develops and primes new brain networks. Hence, it makes it easier for one to learn even more languages.

That said, picking up a new language is certainly not easy. It requires (   ), patience, time, and a great deal of practice. Moreover, joining a paid tutoring program that offers certification can be expensive. Despite its challenges, learning a foreign language is a beneficial life skill. It helps define one's future (   ) and shape one's perspective in this ever-evolving world. Ultimately, the secret to commanding a foreign language depends on how proficiently a person can speak and understand his or her mother tongue.

(lexicon, multilingualism, passionate, dialects, nativism, predominance, proficient, cognitive, dedication, aim)

The most (   ) activity a person can engage in is sleeping. It is an essential biological function that plays a vital role in the (   ) and (   ) of our minds. Thus, it directly affects happiness, mood, memory, and concentration. The precise reason why we sleep is still unclear, and the question remains a mystery in health science. The biological function of sleep is one of the very few scientifically proven explanations.

Sleep is the practice of closing our eyes and letting the body and brain rest and recharge for the day ahead. This may sound like a simple thing, but it is significant for the functioning of our bodies. According to the National Center for Biotechnology Information, within a minute after going to bed, noticeable changes occur in the brain and body. Our temperature and heart rate drop because our energy consumption is lower during this period. In this process, the brain cells send electrical signals and release (   ) chemicals. As a result, the body and brain both have time to rest for the busy day ahead.

Some say that sleep releases one's wildest thoughts and dreams. While we sleep, brain cells send electrical signals back and forth to each other. These include recent memories being converted into long-term memory through the (   ) path. While doing so, they (   ), bump into each other, and strange images are seen in dreams.

Think of this process: Our brain is like a film director, writer, and actor all in one. How long does a human need to sleep on average to enjoy these homemade movies? The amount depends on one's age. Adults aged 18 to 60 require at least 7 hours, and those who do not get enough of it may easily suffer from (   ) such as being short-tempered and tired. (   ), a lack of sleep may interfere with work concentration, impoverishing a person financially and physically.

Finally, sleeping trouble is a universal problem. Try this habit: Avoid screen time at least two hours before bed and wake up at the same time to establish a (   ). Even sleeping on one's stomach can help one fall asleep quicker. After all, maintaining physical, mental, and financial health is a practice. The individual is responsible for creating or destroying his or her own life. In this context, thus, sleeping plays a very meaningful role.

(astonishing, formation, enrichment, healing, neural, collide, strange, symptoms, Ultimately, routine)

The "space business" is an umbrella term for space-related enterprises. This industry aims to help humans by providing communication services, navigational tools, climate (   ), spying, and more. In the past, this business was operated by and for the armed forces. Now it is mainly done by private companies and governments of developed countries with local, highly skilled human capital. The data generated by these businesses are used for defense and commercial purposes.

Historically, humans were not able to realize their ambitions of controlling space. These (   ) had existed since 1957, when the Soviet Union launched the first artificial satellite, Sputnik, into orbit. In 1962 NASA sold space to private (   ) for commercial satellites to tap the promising economy full of opportunities. Nevertheless, failures were common until the 1970s, when launch technology became reliable. Things have certainly changed over the years. In 1986, after the Challenger space shuttle exploded, NASA stopped launching projects. Later, the Pentagon became a new customer of private launch firms.

Today, the (   ) enterprise is enjoying a (   ) in popularity. Many private organizations worldwide, including in China, successfully launch rockets with human crews into the (   ). Since 1993, India has launched 342 foreign satellites for 34 countries via its Polar Satellite Launch Vehicle. India ranks fifth among all countries in the world regarding space tech businesses and is becoming a hub for small satellites. The government of India has opened this business to private players. As a result, 350 ventures are developing low-cost solutions on par with global powers.

Like their Cold War (   ), these Asian giants have specific aims and a thirst for publicity. Japanese companies are already supplying robots and satellite tools. This type of business is undoubtedly (   ), with global (   ) nearing $385 billion. Economists expect revenues to be in the trillions of dollars by the middle of this century. This industry is creating various tech industry jobs, benefiting the world economy and human well-being.

Nevertheless, space (   ) has encountered emerging problems, such as cosmic debris. Moreover, at present, we are unable to move past geopolitical rivalries. These conflicts continue to affect approaches to outer-space exploration. To resolve those issues, we need to remove geopolitical hurdles and increase the collaborative study of the cosmos. The day is not far when our children or grandchildren will tell us that they are heading out on a space excursion from school the following week.

(forecasts, aspirations, entities, interplanetary, rise, cosmos, ancestors, lucrative, revenues, exploration)

Passport (   ) refers to the ability of the passport holder to travel and enter various countries without restrictions. The importance of a passport cannot be (   ). With globalization and technological advancements, there have been some significant changes.

Strong passports such as those from Canada (184) and the United States (185) allow their citizens to travel visa-free around the world. According to the global citizenship and residence advisory firm Henley & Partners (2021), some of the most (   ) passports are those of Japan, Singapore (192), Germany, and South Korea (190), among others. Meanwhile, weaker passports, such as those of Afghanistan (26), make traveling abroad much more difficult because travelers face a visa barrier. In this context, nations often grant visa exemptions because reducing paperwork can bring in (   ) flows of (   ) foreigners. Streams of people bring economic benefits in various forms and improve the status of a country with its peers. The receiving country considers several critical factors before granting visa exemptions for specific nations, such as the economic position of the sending country, (   ), and refugee flows.

Regardless of a person's passport, the (   ) thing is whether it can be used to access education. A powerful passport will be easier to use to enter higher education or find employment abroad. In the case of Japan, the country with "the world's most (   )passport," only 24% of citizens are passport holders, the lowest proportion among rich countries. Most people feel uncomfortable with the idea of experiencing a new world. Several factors prevent them from traveling, including limited annual leave, food restrictions, (   ) concerns, and safety. Most importantly, there is fear of discomfort from not being understood. In recent days, even retired pensioners, who have abundant free time and money, travel less than their parents. Until the 1990s, Japanese people were excited to (   ) the world. Youths took a month- or week-long tour with copies of *Chikyu No Arukikata* (How to Walk the Earth), a favorite travel guide. All because a strong yen made their journey practical and possible.

The increasing cost of studying abroad (approximately $30,000 annually) no longer represents an inexpensive deal for Japanese families. Indeed, wealthy, highly educated parents know the benefits of using a passport to study abroad for financial stability. The ability to study and gain work experience abroad is entirely dependent on what passport one has, i.e., one's citizenship. According to Forbes magazine 2017, 42% of citizens in the US and 76% of people in England held a passport. It shows how citizens' lifestyles change with exploration or their willingness to experience the world.

In general, many politicians and people in business prefer that their children study abroad. Building human capital from an early age provides lifetime assets. Business deals and political ties are based on trust, and the period people know each other. After all, holding something powerful and making the best use of it is a real strength.

(strength, overstated, powerful, steady, deep-pocketed, diplomatic ties, most important, powerful, hygiene, wander)

18

Fake news is a universally present and (   ) concept in the internet age. Today, political parties, news outlets, and (   ) groups have no morals about spreading misinformation. Anyone on the internet can broadcast made-up "facts" with no verified sources or quotations.

Contrary to popular belief, the concept of fake news is not novel. The word "misinformation" has been around since the late 16th century. The spread of those types of news was (   ) in the early modern period and was an essential issue for the leading philosophers of the era. For example, Francis Bacon discussed the dangers of confirmation bias in his Novum Organum (1620).

Today, the body of false news is (   ) than that of actual news stories. Those who spread these false stories often base them on personal beliefs, making it more challenging to separate fact from fiction. Fake news often uses deliberately (   ) and aggressive language to hide the fact that it is falsified.

First, such news exists within a complex ecosystem of disinformation and misinformation. These stories are often twisted and broadcast by political parties and policymakers to (   ) public opinion. Misinformation is inaccurate statistics or facts mistakenly spread by undisciplined journalists without the intent to cheat. With the help of technological convenience, such content can easily be spread by sharing it on social media, blogs, and sites such as Wikipedia.

Second, bots and websites that publish (   ) content also spread half-truths. Economically driven gossip sites and platforms use false statements to generate clicks. The internet has also (   ) long-refuted (   ), such as the flat earth theory. The internet makes it easy to find fanatics and (   ) them as they form online communities.

In conclusion, relying on verified sources in such confusing times is critical. One must use reputable publications to fact-check data, as this is the only way to reduce the wide broadcasting of fake news. Ultimately, everyone is free to judge, analyze and think independently. The final judgment or decision varies from person to person depending on the individual's analytical skills, ethnicity, family background, and wisdom.

(notorious, propaganda, rampant, denser, sensitive, sway, clickbait, revived, conspiracies, deceive)

About the author,

Dr. Abhay has been involved in education since 2011 as a Professor and writer. He has taught various subjects like Japan and the West from an Asian Perspective. In addition, Indian Consumption and Consumerism from a Cross-Cultural Perspective.

Abhay is the author of 3 books and various academic papers. His papers have been published in reputed international journals and have been read at several prestigious international conferences.

He has a Ph.D. from Kobe University, Japan. In his student life, he has won the Japanese language speech contest five times, conducted in different states of Japan.

His teaching philosophy emphasizes acquiring a knowledge base. He strongly believes in the significant role played by one's mother tongue. His 21 years of international stage experience says that learning a foreign language is always easier with mastery of one's mother tongue. Living in a foreign land is always challenging. People may deny you very often, but that itself becomes your stepping stone to success.

Reading for a Bright Future   [B-945]
明るい未来を拓く英語リーディング

1　刷　2023年3月13日

著　者　Abhay Joshi　　　　ジョシ　アバイ

発行者　南雲一範　Kazunori Nagumo
発行所　株式会社　南雲堂
　　　　〒162-0801　東京都新宿区山吹町361
　　　　NAN'UN-DO Co., Ltd.
　　　　361 Yamabuki-cho, Shinjuku-ku, Tokyo 162-0801, Japan
　　　　振替口座：00160-0-46863
　　　　TEL: 03-3268-2311（営業部：学校関係）
　　　　　　　03-3268-2384（営業部：書店関係）
　　　　　　　03-3268-2387（編集部）
　　　　FAX: 03-3269-2486

編集者　加藤　敦

表　紙　銀月堂

組　版　Office haru

検　印　省　略

コード　ISBN978-4-523-17945-0　C0082

Printed in Japan

E-mail　nanundo@post.email.ne.jp
URL　https://www.nanun-do.co.jp/